PSYCHOLOGY AND TEACHING

PSYCHOLOGY
AND TEACHING

by

H. S. N. McFARLAND M.A. B.Ed.

LECTURER IN EDUCATION
UNIVERSITY OF ST ANDREWS

GEORGE G. HARRAP & CO. LTD

LONDON TORONTO WELLINGTON SYDNEY

First published in Great Britain 1958
by GEORGE G. HARRAP & CO. LTD
182 High Holborn, London, W.C.1

Reprinted by photo-lithography: 1960; 1963

Composed in Baskerville type and printed by
Lowe & Brydone (Printers) Limited
London, N.W.10
Made in Great Britain

Contents

Chapter		*Page*
1.	THE SCOPE OF EDUCATIONAL PSYCHOLOGY	7
2.	ANIMAL LEARNING AND HUMAN LEARNING	18
3.	LEARNING AND REMEMBERING	28
4.	INTELLIGENT THOUGHT AND ACTION	45
5.	EDUCATIONAL ASSESSMENTS	66
6.	EDUCATIONAL BACKWARDNESS	82
7.	DISCIPLINE, DELINQUENCY, AND DEPRIVATION	96
8.	ÆSTHETIC AND TECHNICAL EDUCATION	111
9.	PERSONALITY	128
10.	INFANCY AND CHILDHOOD	143
11.	ADOLESCENCE AND MATURITY	154
12.	MENTAL HEALTH	167
13	A BIOLOGICAL VIEW OF MAN	179
14.	A SOCIAL VIEW OF MAN	194
15.	THE PSYCHOLOGIST AND THE EDUCATOR	209
	BIBLIOGRAPHY	219
	INDEX	227

Diagrams and Tables

Fig.   *Page*

1. THE USUAL GROUPING OF INTELLIGENCE
   QUOTIENTS   51

2. DISTRIBUTION OF OCCUPATIONAL CLASS FOR
   CHILDREN SCORING SIXTY OR MORE IN THE
   TEST   56

3. OCCUPATIONAL CLASSIFICATION OF FATHERS
   OF TERMAN'S GIFTED CHILDREN   57

4. CALCULATING THE VARIANCE   68

5. NORMAL DISTRIBUTION CURVE   73

6. CORRELATION OF INTELLIGENCE TEST SCORES
   AND UNIVERSITY MARKS   77

7. A SIMPLE BIOSPHERE   141

8. A SOCIOGRAM   202

Acknowledgments

I should like to acknowledge the assistance received in the preparation of this book from Professor J. W. L. Adams and my wife. Dr R. R. Rusk read the proofs and made many useful suggestions.

I also acknowledge my debt to those from whose writings I have quoted. All such sources are included in the bibliography.

H. S. N. McFARLAND

Chapter One

The Scope of Educational Psychology

EDUCATIONAL PSYCHOLOGY begins with the observations and spontaneous questions of people confronted with certain facts of the world. A student finds that there are more books than he has time to read, that new words and ideas are freely used before he completely understands them, and that new freedoms bring their own problems and responsibilities. He thinks about these problems, discusses them with his fellows, and searches for clues in the comments of lecturers. The wiser learn gradually how to select the best from books, how to note the salient facts and arguments of lectures, how to use reference books, and how to record observations and experiments. They improve, not only by acquiring good techniques of study in the narrower sense, but by acquiring deeper insight into their own personalities. They progress, in fact, by solving the problems of their own educational psychology.

Similarly, a young teacher beginning to work with children faces another and wider range of problems in educational psychology. His well-conned knowledge, his carefully prepared lesson, his expectations of how the children will behave—all may be shattered by the infinite variety and waywardness of real children. They may be intellectually incapable of understanding what is taught. They may be bored by the manner of its teaching. They may not have had time to grow accustomed to the new teacher. They may, however, be delighted and respond beyond the novice's most optimistic hope. Whatever happens, and at whatever academic level, the teacher cannot avoid the recurrent problems of educational psychology: What can I expect of children of different ages? How widely do children of the same age vary? How far does it depend on their education at home and how far on what they inherit? How can I interest them and make them learn? How do I cope with the dull or backward and with the very bright? What is to be done with naughty children? How do I keep discipline? Do I.Q.s really show how intelligent or unintelligent they are? How wide is the teacher's responsibility? Am I to concern myself with the whole development of the child or can I reject responsibility for the non-scholastic aspects? These are typical of the questions to which educational psychologists have offered answers.

As a separate study, educational psychology belongs to the twentieth century, although it has strong roots going back to Rousseau in the eighteenth century. And, of course, even before that people could not help having some educational psychology. For centuries learning by heart and discipline by corporal punishment were central principles of educational practice. Neither is so unquestioningly accepted to-day, although each can still muster defenders, just as in times long past there were some advocates and practitioners of a tolerant humanistic attitude which we perhaps too hastily arrogate to modern education. The study of the history and philosophy of education gives a useful perspective to educational psychology. Political, religious, and philosophic considerations are always so intermingled with educational problems that one cannot easily disentangle purely psychological factors. For the purposes of analytical study the disentanglement must be attempted.

Anyone who has studied the history of scientific progress knows that the most practically useful results do not always emerge from inquiries that are meant to be practical. A revolution at the level of theory has often been the pre-cursor of many useful applications. One of the best-known modern examples is the way in which the theoretical study of the atomic nature of matter was the prelude to atomic bombs and nuclear power stations. Similarly, in the field of educational psychology it is not the most obviously practical devices—intelligence tests, new reading books, or child-guidance clinics—that are necessarily of greatest practical importance. The argument of this book will be that there are different levels of practicality. The earlier chapters will discuss learning and remembering, intelligence and educational assessments, discipline and delinquency, and the more recent emphasis on the æsthetic and technical sides of school education; these matters are practical in the most obvious and commonly used sense. The middle chapters will review some of the approaches to the psychology of personality and of child development; a teacher's views on these topics determine how he solves the more obvious practical problems of learning and discipline. Finally, in the last chapters it will be argued that a general under-standing of the nature of man, and particularly of oneself, is not of academic interest only but is also the most widely practical part of educational psychology.

If educational psychology is a separate subject of study it should have a fairly definable field of its own, a recog-nized body of literature, and recognized methods of systematic study. These requirements can be met. Some of the topics of study are the physical, intellectual, emotional, and social development of young people; methods of learning and teaching; techniques of assessing abilities, aptitudes, and attainments; and the problems of backward-ness, delinquency, and maladjustment. For each of these there is a large and important recent literature, and in some cases writings dating from the late nineteenth or early

twentieth century which, for a young study like educational psychology, are classics. A casual selection of recent
works would include the American *Manual of Child
Psychology* (1954), edited by Carmichael, Gesell's detailed
studies of child development, Terman's studies of gifted
children, Burt's studies of backwardness and delinquency,
Schonell's studies of specific backwardness, the Scottish
Research Council's *Social Implications of the 1947 Mental
Survey* and other careful statistical studies, Valentine's
publications on educational psychology, and many books
stemming from the psychoanalytic movement. Among the
'classics' one might include Francis Galton's *Hereditary
Genius* (1869), James Sully's *Studies of Childhood* (1895),
William James's *Talks to Teachers on Psychology* (1899),
Stanley Hall's *Adolescence* (1904), Binet's individual scales
of intelligence, and McDougall's *Introduction to Social
Psychology* (1908).

These are some of the outstanding works. In addition,
each main problem of educational psychology subdivides
into subsidiary problems, some of which are extensive in
scope. Much time and labour and thought are required to
construct a good objective test. Statistical methods are
essential for the solution of many problems and are complex in their own right. Child-study demands long, patient,
skilled observation. The more thorough the observations of
individual cases, the more difficult it is to study a sufficiently large group to establish any generalization. If a large
representative group is studied it may be possible to make
only a few observations of each individual. A specialist
immersed in any of these topics, like the student confronted
with one specific text-book, is liable to conclude : "This is
educational psychology!" But educational psychology
comprises all of these special studies, linked on the one
side to general psychology and on the other to the practical
work of education. General psychology strives to perceive

more abstract and general patterns in human behaviour and experience. Practical education often demands more immediate and speedy solutions and is understandably impatient of what cannot be used here and now.

The third criterion to be satisfied is that educational psychology should have recognized methods of systematic study. Four such methods may be mentioned. Firstly, this century has seen an increased recognition of the importance of more accurate observations of children's behaviour. This has been done (a) by making records on paper, magnetic tape, or photographic film, at the time of the observation, before the passage of time plays tricks with our memories; (b) by observing one or only a few kinds of behaviour at any time, so that observations do not become impossibly complicated; and (c) by controlling the circumstances in which the observations are made, so that, for example, a child is not inhibited by the presence of an anxious parent or by the critical comments of an untrained observer.

Secondly, there has been an increased recognition of the importance of studying sufficiently big and appropriate samples to establish some notion of what behaviour is typical for any defined class of children, and what proportions deviate from the typical, and by how much and in what direction. It is popular to make fun of 'the average child' and to suggest that there is no such animal. This is only partly justified. Statistical studies are doing with attempted precision just what we all do in our everyday thinking about people. If we take any quality at all, such as honesty, intelligence, manual dexterity, good humour, is it not the case that there is a large proportion of people who possess the quality in a middling degree? They are honest in so far as they would not, of course, deliberately cheat us, although they might pocket an uncollected bus fare or forget about a bill that some creditor had accidentally omitted to send. They conduct their affairs with reasonable intelligence, barring some mistakes, and taking into account the limitations or opportunities of their walks of life. They have what manual dexterity they need. They can joke with us upon occasion. And are there not few who strike us by their eminent lack or abundance of such qualities? Does not the very idea of great intelligence take its meaning from being a deviation above the average of human intelligence or the idea of dishonesty from being a deviation below the average of human honesty?

Thirdly, there has been an increased use of experiments to find the answer to various questions. Here the circumstances are controlled as completely as possible and hypotheses, or tentative solutions, put to a more rigorous test. In the educational 'laboratory,' as in the physical scientist's laboratory, the experimental method does not always work with precision. The experimental evidence about educational problems is often complex or incomplete. But experiments have contributed to progress. Recently the effects of giving children practice or coaching in intelligence tests have been experimentally studied. One unsurprising effect is that the children's performances improve. But it seems that the extent of the improvement has limitations which are now more accurately known. In an older and well-known experiment the possibility was tested of training young children to climb stairs and do similar actions either better or earlier than is allowed by the normal, untutored course of development. This revealed that certain skills can be learned efficiently only when the learner has reached the requisite stage of maturity. A good teacher saves much time and effort by taking account of each child's readiness for a particular stage of learning.

And fourthly, there have been continual attempts to make more precisely quantitative assessments of various aspects of human personality and behaviour. The intellectual aspects of personality have been more successfully measured than the temperamental and emotional. It is unfortunate that this part of educational psychology has been called 'mental measurement.' We all prize our intellectual and temperamental individuality so highly that we may resent being placed against the yardstick of an intelligence or a personality test. Who is he who dares to know the secret of human nature? We like to be 'understood' in the sense of 'sympathetically considered,' but we also like to feel that our private lives cannot be reduced to quotients, glandular balances, or subconscious complexes.

Educational psychology itself, despite the achievements just claimed, is not always 'understood.' It has been criticized for dressing plain truths in fancy jargon, for obscuring the genuine values of traditional educational methods and ideals, and for being insufficiently practical. The validity and limitations of such criticisms can be discussed, but it should be noted that the critics have usually been most virulent where they have been least informed. It is equally easy to acquire and to ridicule psychological jargon, but every subject must have its technical terms. If the terms are invented to refer to new ideas the layman feels left in the dark. If some existing word is used to refer to the new idea the layman confuses the new meaning with the old. The idea of intelligence is a good example. Although it is convenient to use 'intelligence' to refer to what is measured by modern intelligence tests, the word has a wider and longer-established sense which includes maturity of judgment and *savoir-faire* as well as the ability to solve intellectual problems. There is no doubt that there is a strong tendency for those who are eminent or deficient in one kind of intelligence to be similarly eminent or deficient in other kinds, but the correspondence or correlation is by no means perfect. There are some brilliant fools, and some wise men of humble intellectual attainments.

The psychological use of the word 'intelligence' is an

example of a well-known term receiving a more specialized meaning for a particular purpose. Psychologists use words such as 'primary reinforcement,' 'goal discrepancy,' 'sublimation,' 'displacement,' or 'closure,' which have little significance for a layman. They are essential, if puzzling, abbreviations. They give names to newly noted relationships, just as the physical scientist finds it easier to talk about 'specific gravity' than to repeat 'the ratio between the weight of a given volume of a substance and the weight of the same volume of pure water at $3.945°$ C.' The difficulty about this use of technical language is that even the long-hand version of the idea may be complex and unfamiliar and, therefore, not easily understood. The important question is whether one achieves a better explanation, and consequently a better control of known events. But what is the test of whether an explanation is better? Mainly, that the explanation should group many facts into a few relationships. These relationships may increase our practical control of events and may lead to new inquiries and discoveries.

Even scientists may cling to traditional patterns and hinder the recognition of the value of new explanations. Professor Beveridge (1950) writes :

It has been said that the reception of an original contribution to knowledge may be divided into three phases : during the first it is ridiculed as not true, impossible, or useless; during the second people say there may be something in it but it would never be of any practical use; and in the third and final phase there are usually people who say that it is not original and has been anticipated by others.

Educational psychology, whatever its misdemeanours, has in practice greatly improved the lot of children, and consequently of those who have to deal with them. Individual differences among children have been carefully mapped. Important distinctions have been drawn between various groups, such as the dull and the bright. Notably, the old assumptions that dull children could easily make up for their dullness in other ways and that bright children tend to be inferior in physique or sociability have been shown to be false. The case for respecting individuality as one of our educational aims has been strengthened in practice by providing the concrete means of catering for varied needs. In part this has been achieved by creating new institutions, new means of assessment, new ways of teaching. But child-guidance clinics, special schools for handicapped children, standardized tests, activity methods, play-ways, and all the rest are only one aspect of the movement. The more subtle and important part is the wider, more complex pattern against which we now see any individual child.

It is common for students, and even teachers, of educational psychology to be carried away by the trappings of the subject. They put their faith in the tests and the jargon and are disappointed and aggrieved when these let them down. But if the more obvious devices of educational psychology have solved problems that were unsolved or ignored in the past a more critical consideration of what we have learned reminds us that we are not the first who have warmed sympathetically to the problems of the young. Nor have we gone far in solving some of the biggest problems. Both points can be illustrated.

In the second half of the sixteenth century James Melville was born near Montrose, on the east coast of Scotland. His mother died when he was an infant, and he owed what maternal affection he received to various foster-mothers. He was educated in the stern morality and dour theology of the Presbyterian reformers. His practical, hard-headed father intended to put him to farming, but was persuaded to give his son an education at local schools and at the University of St Andrews. James grew to manhood deeply imbued with a sense of God's omnipresence in the world of man and keenly interested in learning and divinity. This sounds a far cry from the child-centred world of modern educational psychology. Yet in his autobiography Melville testifies in convincing terms to the loving concern of his father, to the lavish provision of sporting activities at school, to the thrill of boyhood games and pranks, to the kindly ministrations of his tutor at the university, and to the lively intellectual stimulus of his uncle Andrew's 'post-graduate' tuition. Here was a warmly humane education flourishing among dour` people who would have been astonished by the theories of modern educational psychologists.

Turning our eye from the past to the present, we can instance a problem which neither humane feeling nor psychological theory has completely solved, From 1927 child-guidance clinics began to be established in this country. They have done a great service in diagnosing, and sometimes remedying, educational backwardness and retardation, and childish delinquencies. But the problems they diagnose are often the deep, stubborn problems of a badly organized community or of selfish and irresponsible families. The psychologist's ministrations alone cannot solve moral and social problems that depend for their solution upon the continual intimate relationships within family groups and between neighbours in a community. This reminds us that psychological understanding can remain at an intellectual level without translating itself into the delicate interplay of conversation and activity which really enables people to live happily together. The details of human problems change radically, but, whatever the circumstances, there remains the eternal problem of living happily together.

Educational psychology might be defined as the systematic study of human behaviour and experience in relation to the problems of educating people. It is scientific in some respects that have been discussed earlier, but its quantities are perhaps too uncertain, its observations too mixed up with educational theories, and its data too refractory, for it to be called a science in the sense of the physical sciences. But those parts that are not fully scientific may still be fascinating and rewarding to the individual student. While learning about I.Q.s and reliabilities and validities, a student should spend some time with children of different ages and I.Q.s, asking what 'intelligence' means in relation to their sayings and doings. While delving into studies of delinquency, he should meet some delinquents in order to find out how 'normal' some of them are, and should reflect on which delinquencies are grave and which trivial. And the teacher whose study of educational psychology makes him feel that "Tout comprendre, c'est tout pardonner" must still decide what is best not pardoned, even if understood. One young teacher could do nothing with his class, for he believed that the children were not responsible for themselves. Since he did not expect them to be responsible, they behaved irresponsibly. More experienced teachers know that children are not completely responsible, but that appropriate degrees of responsibility must be expected in order to be achieved.

Chapter Two

Animal Learning and Human Learning

THE student who will become a teacher has a double concern with the psychology of learning. As a student he has to acquire new skills, understand new problems, and remember many things that will help his work. He is aided by past achievements or handicapped by the lack of some knowledge or skill. He has habits of regular study or hopes for the best from briefer spells of concentrated 'swotting.' He conscientiously memorizes the words of the text-book and the lecturer or trusts in a general grasp of the subject matter and his own ability to reflect upon it. By experience he develops a general idea of his own strengths and weaknesses and of his standing in relation to his fellows. As a teacher he must help children to acquire the skill, understanding, and knowledge appropriate to their different ages and capacities. Their learning problems are like the student's. They too come with past achievements and handicaps, with different habits, with mechanical or intelligent outlooks, with varying notions of what they can do. So much time and effort go into learning that an attempt to understand the process is justified.

Learning is a most varied and complex process. In a sense we are learning all the time. Without going to school or college at all we learn to like or dislike people, to behave confidently or shyly, to avoid being killed on busy streets, to amuse ourselves, and generally to achieve our purposes within the limitations of our given capacities and environment. School and college learning is not entirely different from these other kinds, although it may be more deliberately planned to prepare men to live in particular societies. A society which values traditional academic achievements makes more provision for the teaching of the classics. A society which values scientific and technical progress provides more lavishly for this. Differing degrees of freedom within societies are matched by more or less indoctrination and propaganda in the classroom. Psychology, strictly speaking, is concerned to describe and explain the facts. In practice explanations often point in the direction of particular educational aims.

Before the twentieth century there were people who appreciated some of the subtle human elements that influence learning, but school learning as a whole was regarded in a way that now seems mechanical. Repetition, memorizing, and punishment for failure constituted more of the learning process than they do to-day. Before discussing the inadequacy of such a conception we should examine whether it may be satisfactory in part. Most people would suspect that sheer practice must have some important place in learning. The problem has been studied with reference to animals, for their learning is not complicated by conscious purpose and they lend themselves more readily to experiments. Some study of animal learning gives a biological foundation to the more practical discussion of human learning.

The whole animal world is capable of 'learning.' The very simplest microscopic organisms may change their stereotyped behaviour temporarily if they receive some stimulus that is adverse to that behaviour. At a higher level, the earthworm's tendency to avoid the light has been used to 'teach' it to turn one way rather than another in the simplest kind of maze. The Russian physiologist Pavlov

(1849-1936) investigated certain elementary kinds of learning by dogs—the kind known as conditioned learning. The smell of food causes saliva to flow into the dog's mouth. We say that salivation is the natural response to the natural stimulus of food. Pavlov regularly preceded the presentation of the food by the sounding of a bell. After a number of repetitions of this sequence the bell alone, with no ensuing food, brought saliva to the dog's mouth. We call the bell a conditioned stimulus.

Many experiments like those by Pavlov have been carried out, and our knowledge of conditioning has increased. But also the word 'conditioned' is misused to describe any learning. The teacher 'conditions' John to like or dislike arithmetic. Mary's manners are 'conditioned' by her upbringing at home. This is misleading. Pavlov was concerned with the mechanics of a physiological situation. Can we regard human beings, with their intelligent awareness of events, in the same manner? The difference in complexity alone is important. Even with dogs Pavlov required great ingenuity to eliminate extraneous influences. A stray odour or some internal excitement in the dog might render an experiment invalid. Only in infancy is human nature near to being as physiological as the dog's.

The pattern of conditioned learning in animals still has relevance to human learning. It suggests that learning should be related to some rewarding situation. The dog's conditioned response to the bell soon fades out if the food reward is permanently withheld. So the child's co-operation with the teacher will evaporate if the rewards of success and approval are permanently withheld. The dog's response may be altered by some stimulus from outside. So the child's attention is readily distracted by the novelty of a classroom visitor or a passing jet aircraft. The dog's response will weaken and disappear as the reward is farther removed in time. So the teacher is advised to give due praise soon after a successful performance. The dog will not be interested in bells if the food has already been presented. So the child may be less interested in work when the examinations which have been presented as the goal are over. The mature student can work for smaller or less concrete rewards. He can tolerate longer delays and reject greater distractions. But perhaps his learning too is governed by the principles just listed.

Pavlov conditioned a dog to respond in one way to a circular shape and in another to an elliptical shape. He then presented intermediate shapes which were increasingly difficult to distinguish as circles or as ellipses. The dog broke down and could not cope with this impossible situation. This is matched by the student's confusion or rebellion when he cannot make sense of a difficult problem. It suggests the importance of making clear distinctions remembering that the clearness must be in the eyes of the learner. Any teacher can see the difference between 'cut' and 'cat,' but some children simply cannot. Grammatical or mathematical distinctions which are clear to an Honours graduate need not be, and often are not, clear to a school certificate candidate.

The American psychologist E. L. Thorndike (1874-1949) was one of the first to experiment extensively in animal learning. In two typical experimental situations a hungry cat had to find its way out of a puzzle-box to get food outside, and a hungry white rat had to find its way through a maze to the food-box at the end. Here we still have a reward situation and the motivation of physical need, but the interest is centred on learning to solve a complex problem. The cat made random movements and eventually operated the mechanism that opened the cage. On subsequent trials the random movements were eliminated. The rat explored the maze and, on repeated trials, went into fewer and fewer blind alleys. At last it could go to the food-box by the shortest route. How were the wrong movements eliminated?

One account suggests that the animal must be motivated by some *drive*, such as hunger. To get rid of the tension associated with the unsatisfied drive, the animal tries various responses. One, or several, of these responses may bring the reward within reach. Having experienced the association of the reward with response A, the animal will tend to repeat A on future occasions. Response A is said to be 'reinforced' by the successful outcome. But, in addition, the animal will tend to associate the reward with other elements in the first experience of success. The white rat will associate the food not only with the last turn in the maze before the food-box was reached but also with all the previous turns in the maze. The spread of the reinforcement to earlier responses is called 'secondary reinforcement.' Eventually you have only to put the rat at the beginning to see it make unerringly towards the food-box at the end. With much practice the animal will take the correct turn at each corner of the maze, not in response to external stimuli (what it sees, smells, and touches) but to kinesthetic stimuli, the nerve impulses from the muscles to the central nervous system. A human example would be the man who takes the correct turning into the street where he lives, even though his eyes are glued to the sporting page of the newspaper as he walks along.

But a complication was discovered. Animals trained to run a maze could still do so when they had been operated on in such a way that they had to use different muscles. Animals that had learned to wade through a maze of shallow water still found the way when, using different muscles, they had to swim through the same maze of deep water. This suggests that animal learning is more than muscular conditioning. One might be tempted to say that the animal 'knows' its way about the maze. The American psychologist E. C. Tolman has supported this view by showing that rats, even if receiving no food, improved their maze-running with time. When food was introduced to reward their efforts they quickly became as efficient maze-runners as those who had been rewarded all the time. Tolman's theory has been called *the sign-learning theory*, for even animal learners seem to profit from the signs of what is a correct solution.

The significance of these animal experiments for education is fourfold. Firstly, even in elementary learning there is more than a simple mechanical process. An awareness of the signs of the situation and a correct orientation seem to enter into successful learning. Children get on to the right or wrong track according to their own intelligence and the skill of their teachers.

Secondly, they make a certain degree of progress even without strong motives. But, rewarded by the prospect of a visit to the local theatre, of the publication of their best literary efforts in the class magazine, of a visit to France, or just by a word of approval, the children may apply themselves more whole-heartedly to dramatic and literary studies, to history, geography, or the French language.

Thirdly, the possibility of transferring learning from one situation to another is illustrated in some of the animal experiments. In human learning such transfer is not always automatic, but teachers can do something to encourage it. They may, for example, encourage a conscientious approach to work in general by showing their approval in specific instances. They may suggest that the accepted features of good English can be embodied in translations from a foreign language as well as in essays for the English teacher. Such transfers have to be encouraged, for human beings readily segregate different parts of their own learning.

Fourthly, animal-maze learning, or trial-and-error

learning, is comparable with human learning in problematical situations. The outsider, like the psychologist looking
down on the maze, may see clearly the route to a solution.
Hence the value of consulting some one in a relatively
independent position, as the student may consult his tutor
or a pupil the careers master. But the learner in the 'maze'
does not see the whole pattern and must experiment in
order to reach the goal. Learning to translate from a
foreign language has some trial-and-error features. Several
meanings of a word may have to be tried out before one
of them makes sense in the context. Mathematical problems may take one into wrong alleys before the true path is
found. The child who is not ready to understand what a
fraction is may not get away from the idea that, since $\frac{1}{4}$ has
a 4 in it, the fraction must be bigger than $\frac{1}{3}$. Adults can
experience this 'in-the-maze' feeling by tackling such
favourite problems as how to transport three cannibals and
three missionaries across a river, given that the boat holds
only two and that no missionary must ever be alone with
more than one cannibal.

Animal experiments of the kind described hitherto have
been used extensively to support the theory of 'behaviourism.' This theory has appeared in various forms, but
essentially it consists in explaining behaviour as far as
possible in terms of its observable manifestations without
reference to inner thoughts and emotions. The *Gestalt*
theory, on the other hand, has stressed the part played in
learning by the way we perceive things. *Gestalt* is the
German word for 'shape.' The main thesis of this school of
psychology is that the shape or configuration of things
largely determines our perceptions and learning. The
Gestalt law of Prägnanz states that we tend to perceive
the world in terms of simplicity, symmetry, and uniformity.
The moment we begin to perceive or learn something,
argue the *Gestalt* psychologists, we tend to see the some-

thing as a whole. Earlier animal experiments often eliminated the possibility of seeing the problem as a whole. Köhler (1925) got apes to solve problems in which they could see the whole field of the problem, not just two alternative alleys in a maze. For example, the apes might have to learn that two sticks could be joined together to pull bananas into a cage from outside. Or they might have to use boxes to reach food hanging from a high point in the cage. Köhler found that, in such situations, learning was not always by trial-and-error. The apes sometimes saw the solution in a moment and put it into immediate effect. This suggested that learning by 'insight' had some biological foundation in the animal world and was not a human prerogative. Köhler also found that animals, like men, vary in their ability to learn.

The teacher often seeks to produce learning by insight in his pupils. He tries to put things into such a configuration that the children will see why something is the case. The children, of course, like Köhler's apes, vary in their capacity to perceive new configurations. But the configurations must be manipulated to give them the greatest intelligibility.

One kind of configuration is based on *similarity*. We perceive all the red blocks as one group and all the yellow blocks as a second group, although red and yellow may be mixed up as they lie. So the language teacher groups together words or idioms that resemble one another in some point of usage, or the arithmetic teacher gives many sums which embody the same group of number combinations, or the biologist groups small-winged birds together to illustrate a common principle of flight.

A second type of configuration is by *proximity*. A group of diverse objects are seen as one group because they are near to one another. Grammar-school studies may be thought to constitute a distinct type of education, although the products of such studies may be diverse in themselves and not entirely distinct from the products of other educational groups.

A third type is based on *continuity*. The chimpanzee who conceived a continuity between two separate sticks and a food reward outside the cage was able to obtain the food. The educational relevance may be that the means of reaching the goal must appear in convincing relationship to the goal itself. The grammatical study of a foreign language should point towards the actual problems of reading or speaking the language and these, in turn, towards a desired achievement, whether practical or academic.

A fourth principle is that of *inclusiveness*. Just as the scientist deliberately seeks for widely inclusive intellectual views, so we all tend at a simpler level to perceive the most comprehensive patterns. We can listen to the first violins and the second violins, and the flutes, and the bassoons, and all the other parts of an orchestral sound, but we tend to hear the symphony as a whole. So a child, beginning the geography of France, may be aware in turn of the existence of a map on the wall, of the fact that it is a coloured map, and that it contains a certain shape which is labelled France, before he perceives that the brown mass in the bottom right corner represents mountains, that the great river running down beside them is the Rhône, and that Marseilles is near the mouth of it. In college it is useful if students are given a broad conspectus of their studies rather than plunged without guidance into several separate rivulets.

Familiarity makes us readier to perceive those patterns that we know. But a teacher may introduce new ideas by linking them to established ideas. He lets the class air their knowledge, and thus revives their familiarity with a topic before leading them on to new material. In developing the new material he seizes any opportunity of relating it to the children's own experiences. A child who is keen on photography or stamp-collecting or machinery or books may appreciate more quickly the science or geography or literature presented by the teacher. Teachers who encourage such general interests give themselves a better basis for teaching. Everyone, of course, cannot be interested in everything.

Motivation, rewards, and well-ordered training are important in learning, but the *Gestalt* view stresses, in addition, the perception of certain kinds of pattern as clues to learning. The teacher has to take stock of a child's abilities, attainments, and interests so that he can lead him on to perceive new patterns, encouraged on his way by the perception of similarities and continuities. The *Gestalt* emphasis on dramatic improvements in learning, caused by sudden insight into the nature of problems or by perceiving things in a new relationship, has a special appeal to us. Human beings do experience such sudden illuminations. But acceptance of the *Gestalt* interpretation need not be inconsistent with all behaviourism. The *Gestalt* view may be a broad, general account of what the behaviourist analyses into detailed studies of behaviour and physiology. There are more complexities to learning theory than are suggested in this chapter, but these do not lead one nearer to the classroom.

Chapter Three

Learning and Remembering

ROM a practical point of view there are three main problems in human learning. They are the problems of individual differences, of motivation, and of organizing suitable methods and curricula. We recognize that different people have different capacities and we try to assess these as accurately as possible; we recognize that people will do better what they feel some point in doing; and we recognize that any prolonged or complex learning has to be organized into appropriate lessons with appropriate aids, such as books, experiments, or tests, to ensure a successful conclusion. A teacher helping children to learn, or a student trying to learn by himself, has to remember all three aspects if success is to be achieved. There is no point in attempting something that is entirely beyond the learner's capacity, nor in mustering enthusiasm without a plan of study, nor in having a wonderful system of study without any feeling of absorption.

Real progress has been made in mapping the variety of individual differences. Whatever reservations may have to be made about modern tests, they have given us a more accurate idea of how wide the range of ability is at any given chronological age, and have enabled us to say more accurately how much better or poorer than the average a particular child is. We can say with more confidence not only that Johnny is dull or bright, but that he is about one or two or three years behind or ahead of the average for his age. Such comparatively accurate measures of individual difference are available for general ability and for some of the specific scholastic abilities, such as reading and arithmetic. They will be discussed in later chapters. Their importance for learning consists in their enabling us to group children into classes, or into groups within classes, in such a fashion that the material and methods match the needs of the different groups.

It is not surprising that the teacher in a classroom tends to look to teaching methods or particular books to solve the learning problems of the pupils. Sometimes a variety of methods and books is tried without success. It may be that the teacher is attempting the impossible—namely, to solve the problems of all by methods that are relevant to only one group. The teacher can create several homogeneous groups and set each group to work at its own level and in its own way, provided (a) that some guidance has been given on the handling of such groups, (b) that the class is not too big, and (c) that intelligent and accepted principles of classifying are used throughout the school. The principles of educational assessment which will be discussed later are not only a means of experimental study. The application of the psychology of individual differences is an essential part of teaching method.

In terms of classroom situations, the range of individual differences means that some children will come to school able to do a little reading, some will be just about ready to make the first beginnings, while others may need one or two years before they are ready to start on any of the more technical reading processes. It means that some twelve-year-olds will be striding ahead with secondary-school studies while others have still to complete their acquisition of basic skills in the three 'R's.' It means that some seventeen-year-olds will have an eye to university scholarships while others wonder whether they will manage to scrape together a useful leaving certificate. And it means that, even in a highly selected class, such as a grammar-school A form, there will be a noticeable spread of ability from top to bottom. It sometimes seems convenient to ignore these individual differences, but common sense suggests that the more they can be catered for, the farther individuals will advance.

Differences in general intelligence are particularly important, for intelligence test scores tend to indicate likely degrees of success in scholastic performance. Differences in home background influence both intelligence test scores and school achievement. The recent consensus of opinion has been that grammar-school success depends partly on a secure and encouraging home background. McLaren (1950) found a definite association between the socio-economic status of children aged $5\frac{1}{2}$ to 7 years and their reading ability. Children from more prosperous homes were more successful in infant reading. It is, of course, a bigger problem to distinguish between the influence of the actual home environment and of what is physically inherited, but, for better or worse, environment and heredity often reinforce one another. The teacher who knows that a child's home is discouraging or lacking in intellectual stimulus knows that the school must either provide the missing ingredients or expect backwardness and failure.

Attention to individual differences is at the heart of good teaching. It goes beyond the use of psychological tests and findings and can become a matter of respecting the total personality of each child. Treated as whole personalities, children are more likely to respond as whole personalities. Recognizing individual differences contributes, then, not only to good organizing of methods and curricula but also to the motivation of the children, who come to feel that their efforts will be respected. Modern psychology did not discover this possibility, but psychological studies of the kind discussed throughout this book have expanded our practical understanding of it. All our practices in educational and vocational guidance move slowly but surely in the direction of paying greater attention to individual differences. Experimental studies suggest that this results in fewer failures and misfits, although we are nowhere near perfection and may never be so.

Motivation is essential for learning to take place. The motivation of human learning is varied and complex, but all those who have studied learning problems agree that success in an activity is vital if a learner is to persist. Adults do not persist in activities that bring *only* failure and recrimination. It is not surprising to find that the history of very unsuccessful child learners is often one of successive failures and punishments and fallings from grace. There is no very conclusive experimental evidence on the virtues of reward and punishment in human learning, for real-life situations are not strictly experimental, and experimental learning is not strictly real-life. It can be said only that the study of the case-histories of successful and unsuccessful learners suggests that more is gained by rewarding successful achievement than by punishing mistakes. This does not mean that all punishment is ineffective, nor that all rewards are effective, but only that where considerations of success predominate there are more chances of retrieving failures. It is a question of keeping the door of success open even to poor learners instead of confirming them in the expectation and habit of failure. This, of course, leads directly back to individual differences, for success can be assured only by giving learners a carefully graded series of tasks matching their individual abilities and stages of progress. This, in turn, suggests the importance of well-designed and -graded books and materials and lessons.

Motivation is not, therefore, a question only of appealing to a list of appropriate motives. Certainly, children like

stories, boys like adventure, adolescents are concerned to
have the social approval of their fellows, infants want the
teacher's personal approval, action appeals more than
words, the extraordinary tends to hold sway over the
ordinary, the concrete and particular command more
attention than the abstract and general, and the personal
fascinates more than what is impersonal. But a prolonged
programme of learning cannot be kept going by these on
their own; they are subordinate principles. The leading
principle requires more time and skill to master. It consists
in ordering the learning process so that the child is led on
by the joy of realizing his own potentialities in a community
which expects him to do so. The climber seeks the summit
because it is there, and so does the child if he is given the
right chances.

A student can often begin to understand the central
principle of learning motivation if he considers his own
higher studies; if he thinks of how he is influenced by his
teacher's comments and attitudes, by the commendation
of an essay or by the criticism of a low examination mark,
and by his own feelings and hopes about the particular
society of which he is, or hopes to be, a member. Children
at their own level feel the same elations and dejections,
and similarly develop notions of what they have in them
and what they can be. To bring out the best is an art.

There is a sense in which motivation must be constantly
renewed. We get jaded and need fresh stimulation.
Children learning numbers need not practise all the time
in the same way. They may learn by playing at teachers
or at shops, or by dice and paper games, as well as by
more traditional practice. Such devices provide variety
and absorption in the task and help to prevent, for example,
the mechanical recitation of tables without the ability
to use particular number facts. In secondary schools more
teachers of English now draw their grammar lessons from

compositions and general reading instead of from segregated grammatical exercises which only the most intelligent can follow. While recognizing the importance of variety, it is also obvious that much motivation is of a habitual nature. Much learning proceeds from the impetus of accumulated habit. The value of habit has long been accepted, and was notably expressed by William James (1892):

> The great thing, then, in all education, is to *make our nervous system our ally instead of our enemy.* It is to fund and capitalize our acquisitions, and live at ease upon the interest of the fund. *For this we must make automatic and habitual, as early as possible, as many useful actions as we can,* and guard against the growing into ways that are likely to be disadvantageous to us, as we should guard against the plague. The more of the details of our daily life we can hand over to the effortless custody of automatism, the more our higher powers of mind will be set free for their own proper work. There is no more miserable human being than one in whom nothing is habitual but indecision, and for whom the lighting of every cigar, the drinking of every cup, the time of rising and going to bed every day, and the beginning of every bit of work, are subjects of express volitional deliberation. Full half the time of such a man goes to the deciding, or regretting, of matters which ought to be so ingrained in him as practically not to exist for his consciousness at all. If there be such daily duties not yet ingrained in any one of my readers, let him begin this very hour to set the matter right.

It is unrealistic to expect that all children, any more than all adults, should be capable of equal enthusiasm for every learning task. But it is worth considering what happens when people are enthusiastic (not necessarily in any exuberant sense). Then they can absorb, seemingly without effort, what uninterested learners cannot acquire even with great effort. The schoolboy labours over his uncongenial recitation but may have an uncanny memory for locomotives or sporting statistics. A holiday abroad may stimulate more effective learning of a language than several years of school study. The sources of such learning may not be easily tapped, but there is one means of creating such absorption, and that is through the infectious enthusiasm of the teacher. But teachers cannot be filled with infectious enthusiasm overnight any more than their pupils can. It seems, therefore, that the kind of absorption or involvement in learning that is most likely to ensure success is, like the motivation of well-ordered and appropriate studies, something that can be achieved only by the expenditure of genuine and prolonged effort. There is no secret of motivating human learning. It takes a little understanding and a lot of hard work.

In more classrooms to-day (especially those for infants) children are moving about as well as sitting still, doing things instead of only listening to lessons, and following topics through their various aspects as well as having reading, writing, and the rest as separate subjects. More children leave the classroom, the school, and even the country itself, to see things for themselves. More co-operative effort is sought in class or school projects. Gardner (1942, 1950) has attempted to test the results of modern methods in infant schools by comparing groups of children educated traditionally with groups educated in modern ways. It is a difficult experiment to evaluate, but the author is satisfied that newer ways produce at least as good results even in scholastic performance, and possibly better results in personal development. These modern methods reflect new psychological conceptions of the nature of children's development and learning.

Successful motivation is not easily ensured, but the factors just discussed may help—(a) an emphasis on reward rather than punishment, (*b*) a careful relation of the stages of learning to the children's abilities so that they succeed more often than fail, (*c*) the establishing of an atmosphere that brings out the best in the learner by treating him as an individual person, (*d*) a judicious blending of variety and routine, and (*e*) the encouragement of unforced absorption in the task in virtue of the learner's natural inclinations or of his self-identification with the teacher's own genuine enthusiasm.

The third aspect of learning is the organization of methods and curricula. Some of the problems have been studied experimentally. As an illustration we may refer to the Scottish Research Council's *Studies in Arithmetic*. Out of nineteen schools, 464 children were taught subtraction by the method of Decomposition :

$$\begin{array}{ll} 84 & 14 \text{ less } 8 = 6; \text{ write } 6; \\ -28 & 7 \text{ less } 2 = 5; \text{ write } 5. \\ \hline 56 & \end{array}$$

Out of twenty-four schools, 842 children were taught subtraction by the method of Equal Addition :

$$\begin{array}{ll} 84 & 14 \text{ less } 8 = 6; \text{ write } 6; \\ -28 & \quad\quad\quad\quad \text{carry } 1; \\ & 2 \text{ plus } 1 = 3; \\ \hline 56 & 8 \text{ less } 3 = 5. \end{array}$$

Children of 8 to 9 and of 10 to 11 were tested for both speed and accuracy in such sums. Those taught to use the method of Equal Addition were better. This does not, of course, end the matter. Cronbach (1954) quotes an American study by Brownell and Moser in which Equal Addition gave slightly better results if the two methods were taught in a mechanical way, but in which Decomposition proved still better if the teaching was meaningful rather than mechanical. This reminds us of the difficulty of controlling the quality of teaching for experimental purposes. The very desire to prove a case may make a teacher excel himself, although his methods may fall flat in less enthusiastic hands. Moreover, children of different ages may benefit from different methods.

Thyne (1954) studied *Patterns of Error in the Addition Number Facts*. He concluded that number practice should be closely related to the diagnosed weaknesses of pupils, and not consist only of general practice which may miss the weak spots. He found that many errors were 'slips' and wondered whether more thorough rote-learning might be more important than is generally admitted. He found with one test that 9 and 6 were commonly confused, and that the answer to $9 + 4$ was commonly given as 5. He advocates the explanation of subtraction in terms of complementary addition. "Thus, four is one of the parts of nine; four and what are nine? four and five are nine! If we take away the four the five is left!"

It is widely accepted now that it may be futile to embark upon acquiring a technical skill, like reading, before a child has the background of linguistic interest and knowledge that is provided in a good home by the general conversation, bed-time stories, and the like. A certain level of general intellectual development is also necessary, and a mental age of 6 or $6\frac{1}{2}$ is commonly mentioned. Taylor (1950) gave an American test of readiness for reading to 114 Scottish six-year-olds entering their second year of schooling. The Scottish children were, on the average, a year ahead of the American standard. This suggests that schooling can advance early reading achievement and that the idea of reading readiness depends partly on educational opinions as well as on the child's intellectual development.

The examples just given must suffice to show how problems of methods have been studied experimentally.

Although it is difficult to achieve conclusive generalizations, such work has influenced teaching practice. Spelling books now contain words that children are known to use rather than lists chosen for their intrinsic difficulty. Reading and arithmetic books are more carefully graded, and new words or number problems are repeated sufficiently often in various settings to let the learner become naturally familiar with them. Many kinds of concrete apparatus are available to give children varied and diverting practice in the basic reading and counting operations. History and geography text-books have more pictures and illustrations designed to give a sense of reality to their study. Films, television, and visits outside school serve the same general aim. More is done to make the content of any lesson palatable and digestible. The provision of education for all has forced us to take stock of the variety and limitations of children's learning capacity.

In the field of organization and methods psychologists have contributed to sound learning by providing help in classifying children into appropriately homogeneous groups, by contributing to the development of soundly graded books and apparatus, and by encouraging methods and devices that impart a greater sense of reality to learning. We see at the end of this section, as was suggested earlier, that one cannot separate the three fields of individual differences, motivation, and organization. Psychological studies do not prove exactly what teachers should do in every situation, but they support certain courses of action rather than others. These preferred directions have been suggested in the preceding discussion.

One of the perennial problems of human learning is whether 'transfer of training' occurs. Does the study of mathematics make one abler to tackle non-mathematical problems? Or do the other problems have to be similar to mathematical problems? Or does the study of mathematics just impart a certain ability to persist at a problem? Will the good mathematician, accustomed to the step-by-step logic of mathematics, show the same step-by-step reasoning when he talks politics or chooses a wife? There is a persistent belief among schoolmasters that certain subjects are really hard and provide a superior mental discipline. Those who are sceptical about this argue that subjects such as mathematics do not make children more intelligent. It is, rather, that their intrinsic difficulty causes them to be done successfully only by those who already are intelligent in a general way. Cole, summarizing American experiments, writes, "the subjects included in a curriculum should either be valued for themselves or else be very closely related to activities so valued, for neither remote transfer effects nor general mental discipline can be given experimental support." Some experiments confirm common sense in suggesting that learning in no matter what subject may be accompanied by strikingly uninformed and illogical thinking in other fields. The learning of one field is most likely to carry over to another when the relationship between the two fields has been carefully studied and cross-relevancies have been explicitly stated. The case for explicitly relating the content and logic of different subjects has been argued particularly with reference to university studies, in which specialization has the greatest opportunities for segregating the various fields of human understanding.

Problems of remembering and forgetting are closely related to those of learning. Hume (1739) makes a clear statement of a traditional view of memory: "It is evident, that the memory preserves the original form in which its objects were presented, and that wherever we depart from it in recollecting anything, it proceeds from some defect or imperfection in that faculty." This view is still held by some people to-day but is gradually being replaced by another, expressed in the following quotation from William James (1892): "Whilst part of what we perceive comes through our senses from the object before us, another part (and it may be the larger part) always comes out of our own mind."

During the last quarter of the nineteenth century and the first quarter of the twentieth there was an emphasis on experimental studies of the more mechanical aspects of memory. Nonsense syllables were used to get rid of the complications of meaningfulness. If one used meaningful words for memorizing, the task would be easier for those who were most familiar with the words. This seemed to be an interference with 'pure memory.' So strong is the human tendency to impose pattern upon events that, in such experiments, the subjects tended to make up their own meanings, to invent associations, or at least to attach a rhythm to the syllables. Myers (1925) discusses the after-images left by sensory experience, the kinds of association that influence memories, and different methods of measuring how much is remembered or forgotten. "The Superiority of Rational Learning" is discussed in only a brief paragraph.

Two psychologists who have made major contributions to a non-mechanical view of remembering are Freud and Bartlett. Freud (1856-1939) argued that we remember or forget what we want to remember or forget. This is a paradoxical expression of the view that there are psychological processes which influence our behaviour, although we may be unaware or partly unaware of them. Freud (1914) illustrated how even everyday slips of the tongue might cast an oblique light upon our unconscious motives. He shows, for example, how partly repressed ambition manifested itself in the young Dr X "who timidly and reverently introduced himself to the celebrated Virchow with the following words: 'I am Dr Virchow.' " It is easy to collect examples of such lapses from ordinary reading and conversation. It is also kind to refrain from embarrassing the victims, for we all succumb at one time or another and can sometimes catch ourselves out in the expression of some unadmitted longing. Such phenomena suggest that remembering is neither a faculty, nor a machine, nor a store-house. It is an aspect of our total psychological functioning. From the first moment we perceive something we tend to fit it into our own way of seeing the world. In the very act of perception we select and reject. And the process continues, so that after some time we have forgotten things we once knew, and remember things that are different from what other people remember of the same situation. Hence springs the conflict of testimony, and the realization that remembering is not passive but dynamic, moving and moulding the world into the established pattern of our minds. In this sense the wish expressed in the *Rubáiyát* is realized:

> Ah Love! could you and I with Fate conspire
> To grasp this sorry Scheme of Things entire,
> Would we not shatter it to bits—and then
> Remould it nearer to the Heart's Desire!

Bartlett (1932) also represents this function as being active rather than passive. Where Freud's account was based on clinical and everyday experience, Bartlett's was based on experimental studies. Using different methods, he studied how people remembered geometrical designs, pictures, and stories. He found that there was typically an 'effort after meaning,' a striving to give some personal or conventional significance to even the most arbitrary or unfamiliar patterns. When a person once thought of some pattern as being a gate or an anchor, then he tended to reproduce the pattern in a way that made it more like a gate or an anchor than it really was. Moreover, he tended to adhere to his own interpretation even when repeatedly shown the original pattern. Different attitudes and interests tended to produce different perceptions, inferences, and recollections.

In one experiment it was found that exclusive reliance on visual images was not a good way of ensuring accurate recall of five photographs which were shown to twenty subjects. Of the twenty, fourteen transposed details from one photograph to another when they recalled them. Outstanding details were particularly liable to be transposed. Thirteen imported details that were not there, the number of such importations being nineteen. When asked a series of specific questions about the photographs all twenty people imported details, and the number of importations was increased by sixty! In a second free description (by only ten of the subjects) another twenty details were invented. And later, in a third free description, another nineteen details were invented. In the face of such evidence, one can hardly think of memory as a static phenomenon. That is why there is something to be said for using the verb 'remembering' rather than the noun 'memory.'

In a second experiment subjects were asked to reproduce, on successive occasions, a North American story of an unfamiliar kind. Awkwardly unfamiliar elements in the story tended to be omitted, or rationalized into a form more meaningful to the subject. Salient features of the story were transposed. The terse style of the story was appreciated but not readily reproduced. The form of the subject's first recollection of the story tended to persist in later recollections.

In a third experiment twenty-two subjects learned three

sets of picture-signs, such as = *strong*. When

the subjects recollected the signs some of the observed tendencies were (a) to ignore details that did not represent something familiar, (b) to make the signs more like conventional signs or pictures, and (c) occasionally to emphasize odd details. Those depending mainly on visual cues to recall the sign language treated each item separately, thought of analogies to help them remember, had incidental but irrelevant associations along with their remembering, and were rapid and confident. Their confidence was often unjustified. Those depending on word cues recalled the name of the sign before the sign itself, used the principle of classification to help them, and were more hesitating, doubtful, and deliberate, though not necessarily less accurate. A few signs were found to be amusing. The sign for philosophy was thought to be appropriate, seeming to represent a great structure on a small foundation. Difficult signs caused displeasure and an attitude of determination to remember, but they still tended to be forgotten.

In the fourth kind of experiment a story was passed from one person to another, rather after the style of the party game. Proper names and titles proved highly mutable; there was a bias towards the concrete; individual characteristics tended to be replaced by the characteristics of the social group to which the subjects belonged; and there were abbreviations, rationalizations, and radical changes of the story.

Bartlett's general conclusion is that remembering is more a matter of actively organizing, than of merely recognizing, something that happened in the past. Appetites, instincts, interests, and ideals "cut across the strict chronological mode of organizing past experience." The part played by sensory images is that of increasing "the chance of variability in the reconstruction of past stimuli and sensations.

Both in perception and recall, the meaning tends to be determined by a few dominant factors.

A person does not simply have a good or bad memory. An impressive command of sporting records and scores is compatible with a poor recollection of French irregular verbs. Apart from factors of interest, however, it is possible for students to improve their memorization to some extent by adopting appropriate methods. There are two main maxims: it is better to practise recalling what has to be memorized rather than to keep the book or the notes too long in front of one; and it is better to make sure that one understands the material and can relate it to what is already known rather than to trust in parrot-learning.

The relevance of modern views of remembering and forgetting to education is clear. Neither school pupil nor college student is to be thought of as containing a learning or remembering machine which will work efficiently if only its possessor applies himself to the task. What seems to be vital is an emotional absorption in the task, together with a critical attitude to one's own performance. When learning or remembering becomes very inefficient (and when the learner is sufficiently intelligent for the task in hand) the aim must be to alter attitudes, to get rid of emotional 'blockages,' rather than to hope for progress through deliberate application and practice *by themselves*. Human functions cannot be isolated. Intellectual and emotional factors are intricately interlocked. Even the teacher, officially concerned with a child in his capacity of learner, must approach him in his total capacity as a human being in order to get the best results. There are various devices, such as vivid presentation, and reference to the learner's existing interests and knowledge, to help him into a new learning situation, but ultimately the learner must become absorbed, not merely titillated. This is illustrated in a study of Forces' Educational Broadcasts described in the *Times Educational Supplement* (1951):

> There was no short way to make a subject interesting which was not intrinsically so; devices advocated by some as substitutes were spurious. They had a negligible influence, except in certain circumstances when they might even be a positive hindrance. Illustrations, dramatic or descriptive, often had the effect of obscuring the point they were intended to clarify.

Chapter Four

Intelligent Thought and Action

N O ONE is more concerned with intelligence than the teacher. He cannot avoid noticing how widely children vary in general and special abilities. Amid talk of bright children and dull children, normal children and slow-developing children, he must ask what exactly we mean by intelligence. Public and private controversy over the use and abuse of intelligence tests will draw him into the contest. Frustrated by his dunderheads, he will ask himself if all is not predetermined by heredity. Conscious of the power of education, he will wonder how far environmental circumstances contribute to the growth of intelligence. The widely different characteristics and educational needs of dull and bright children will compel him to investigate more closely these characteristics and needs. Such insistent problems constitute the framework of this chapter.

'Intelligence' is a vague, general word. It does not refer to a concrete thing but to observable characteristics of thought and action. Like electricity, it is known by its results. One characteristic of intelligent behaviour is that the agent is able to perceive relationships among things and to apply what he perceives in entirely new situations. The less intelligent person is slow to perceive connections and, even when he does, may be unable to apply his understanding in a novel situation. The more intelligent person, on the other hand, understands quickly and can apply his understanding in quite new situations. Also, the more intelligent person is able to handle problems which by their nature are more complex and more abstract, while the less intelligent is limited to simpler and more concrete problems. While some intelligent behaviour is preceded by reasoned deliberation, many kinds of behaviour can be intelligent without being founded on explicit reasoning at the time they occur. Intelligent action can occur on the spur of the moment.

Intelligence is not a matter of all or none, but of more or less. And intelligence is not the only factor present when people adapt themselves to situations. Some people are able to behave intelligently in one situation, but, from emotional causes, are less intelligent in another situation. We can make our own estimates of how intelligent any person is, but the accuracy of such estimates depends upon how long and how well and in what variety of situations we have known the person assessed. Personal estimates are also influenced by our own bias and by the limitations of our own intelligence and experience. This is clearly evident where the *dux* of a primary school shows no exceptional brilliance when matched against the more advanced work and keener competition of a secondary school, or where the bright secondary-school boy proves to be ordinary in university work. Such changes are not typical, but when they do occur they sometimes indicate a too favourable assessment at the earlier stage. It has been shown repeatedly that teachers tend to judge pupils by their absolute achievements, rather than in relation to their different ages and circumstances. Two children may have the same scholastic achievement, but one gets there by 'brains' while the other does so by hard work.

Plato, about two and a half millennia ago, thought of people as having inborn differences in abilities: "There are innate differences which fit them for different occupations." He also believed that the way to the truth was by thinking rather than doing: "Is it not in the nature of things that action should come less close to the truth than thought?" Rousseau, in the eighteenth century, emphasized individual differences and suggested a view of intelligence that has been re-stated in the present century: "Clever men are distinguished from others by their greater or lesser aptitude for the comparison of ideas and the discovery of relations between them." This is the first of two principles stated by the psychologist Spearman some decades ago. He called it the eduction of relations. The second, the eduction of correlates, is the application of a perceived relationship to a further particular example. Suppose one has to find the next two numbers in the series 1, 2, 6, 24, 120 ... The relationship is that of multiplying the first number by 2, the second by 3, and so on. To educe the next two correlates we should multiply 120 by 6, giving 720; then multiply 720 by 7, giving 5040.

Knight (1943) has considered intelligence to be "the capacity for relational, constructive thinking, directed to the attainment of some end." As recently as 1955 Sir Cyril Burt has defended the conception of intelligence as "innate, general, cognitive ability." Without denying the contribution of environment, Burt is emphasizing ability that is inherited rather than acquired, that is manifested in our general functioning rather than in any specialized talents, and that consists in knowing and understanding the world rather than in reacting to it instinctively or emotionally. Intelligence has been equated with g, the common element found in intellectual test results when they are statistically analysed. In the United States the statisticians long tended to avoid the idea of a general intellectual factor, and produced analyses such as Thurstone's, into factors of verbal ability (V), verbal fluency (W), numerical ability (N), spatial ability (S), perceptual ability (P), inductive reasoning (R), and memory (M). Even where British psychologists have associated *g* with a verbal ability factor V or with a practical ability factor F, to give *g*V and *g*F types of intelligence, it is the general factor *g* which has been found to be responsible for most of the variation in test scores. This corresponds to everyday observations by teachers of practical subjects. They find that the boy with the 'better brain' tends to have the 'better hands.' That there are many individual exceptions is undoubted. An extreme case is quoted by Tredgold—"the genius of Earlswood Asylum" who, between 1850 and 1916, resided in the asylum as a mental defective, but who had remarkable skill and inventiveness in carpentry.

Studies by the *Gestalt* psychologists have suggested that the way we 'see' a problematical situation determines to some extent how we deal with it. The chimpanzee that can use a stick to pull a banana into its cage may not 'see' the stick if the stick happens to be the attached branch of a tree. Some intelligent behaviour depends on detaching bits from their usual connection and using them in novel situations. If we start off on the wrong track it is difficult to get back. The elusiveness of a forgotten name is another example of this phenomenon.

N. R. F. Maier carried out various experiments on human reasoning. In one experiment the subjects had to tie together the ends of two cords hanging from different points on the ceiling. One cord could not be reached while the other was held. The room contained tables, chairs, poles, ring-stands, clamps, and pliers. When a person found an easy solution he was urged to search for another solution. Maier was particularly interested in the solution of tying the pliers to one cord and setting them swinging so that one could catch that cord while holding the other. The particular form of intelligence manifested in such solutions clearly depends on reorganizing the world as one knows it; the pliers have to be detached from their pincer contexts and be seen as a dead-weight. An interesting record could be made of such experiences in one's life, noting which original conceptions of a problem are adhered to, and which elements in the situation help a new insight to emerge.

Holloway (1951) considers that intelligent behaviour is characterized by "a capacity for flexibility and adaptation" and that "acts can only be intelligent if they serve a purpose" (not necessarily a conscious purpose; he gives the example of an intelligent climber who may climb intelligently without premeditating his actions).

Intelligence Tests. One of the criteria of intelligence that has been most used and most disputed in modern times is that provided by intelligence tests. The beginnings of such tests are associated particularly with the name of the French physician Binet. The practical problem that faced Binet was that of selecting children for special schools. What he sought was to compile a set of tests which would measure general, innate ability as distinct from specific talents and mainly educational skills. He also sought to avoid the erratic quality that was attached to personal impressions of intelligence, arrived at by casual knowledge of a child. Common-sense judgments provided part of what Binet was after, but these were not usually applied with enough thoroughness and consistency. Binet's first intelligence scale was published in 1905 and was revised in subsequent years. It consisted of a variety of simple practical problems, arranged in groups appropriate to children of different ages. From a child's performance one could assign him a mental age. New versions of this individual test have been produced. Among the more important are the adaptations by Terman and Merrill (U.S.A.), and Burt (London). The scoring of these tests is not completely mechanical, and consistent scoring depends on training and practice.

During the First World War United States Army recruits
were tested with a group test of intelligence. This, the Army
alpha test, could be done by large numbers at the same
time, and could be easily scored. These advantages have
contributed greatly to the increasing use of group tests.
In the United Kingdom they were used mainly for educational purposes until the Second World War, when they
were used to help in the selection of the right men for the
right jobs in the Services. The differing constructions of
individual and group tests are outlined in the chapter on
Educational Assessment.

The material used in intelligence tests can vary consider-
ably, but it is wrong to assume that, because different
materials are used, different kinds of general ability are
being measured. Concrete *objects* may be used, as in Kohs'
Block Design test, in which coloured blocks have to be made
up into patterns of increasing complexity. *Pictures* may be
used, in which the person tested is used to strike out the
odd one; the pictures might be of a cat, a dog, a spade, and
a rabbit. *Words* may be used, as in the analogy test : dry is
to wet as hard is to ... ? *Numbers* may be used, as when
the subject is asked to add to the series 4, 7, 10, 13. ...
Patterns may be used, as in Raven's Matrices; the subject
is shown three-quarters of a pattern; he has a choice of
several fourth quarters with which to complete the pattern;
he has to choose the right one.

Test results are often expressed as intelligence quotients.
In terms of I.Q., Fig. I shows the main dividing lines for
various classification purposes. It must be emphasized that
the apparent precision of the dividing lines is the outcome
of diagrammatic convenience, and not of reality.

Several writers have suggested that this *normal distribution* (as it is technically called) of I.Q.'s results from the
manner of constructing the tests. Burt has maintained that,
on the contrary, an approximately normal distribution of

I.Q.	General Classification	Educational or Occupational Classification	Percentage of Population
130–	Very bright	University, higher technical and professional, academic secondary education.	16
115–129	Bright		
100–114	Upper average	Technical, commercial, general secondary education.	68
85–99	Lower average		
70–84	Dull	Secondary education including 3 'R's.' Semi-skilled or unskilled manual work.	14
50–69	Feeble-minded	Educationally sub-normal.	2
20–49	Imbecile	The best are capable of useful work under supervision. May attend occupation centres.	
0–19	Idiot	The worst need to be cared for completely.	

Fig. I. THE USUAL GROUPING OF INTELLIGENCE QUOTIENTS

intelligence is an observed fact. Burt's view is supported by the common-sense consideration that the general abilities of people do seem to allow themselves more readily to be distinguished in something *like* the pattern of a normal curve.

Psychologists have had regard to the whole range of intellectual ability, from the intellectual development of babies to that of mature adults, and from the gravest degrees of mental deficiency to the heights of intellectual brightness. The Terman-Merrill intelligence scale ranges from the tender mental age of 2 : 6 (two years six months) to the heights of Superior Adult III. The latter suggests (quite without justification) a kind of intellectual superman. Gesell and Griffiths have published developmental schedules for babies. Wechsler, Raven, Heim, and Moray House have produced various tests of adult intelligence. All this work opens up interesting problems. Briefly, one may say that gross mental retardation is detectable in infancy, but that assessments within the main range are very unreliable. Infants are so rapid and varied in their development, and so changeable over short periods in their specific performances, that there is little foundation for any refinement of intellectual discrimination. With adults the complicating factor is experience and learned skills. Adult intelligence, even more than child intelligence, is intertwined with acquired abilities. This leaves open the question of how far these acquired abilities themselves have been fostered by innate capacity and how much by environmental opportunity and stimulus. In practice, tests of adult intelligence have helped to improve the selection of men for various jobs. In scientific studies there have been indications that adult intelligence is maintained best in the realm of knowledge and verbal skill but tends to fall off in quickness of learning and reasoning. Even with adults of outstanding intelligence, substantiality, maturity, and wisdom are expected rather than brilliant intellectual performance alone. Professor Beveridge (1950) has suggested that people tend to fall into the two categories of those who are passive and accept the world as it comes, and "those who habitually react vigorously to external influences," questioning everything and rebelling against the conventional. These categories presumably exemplify a factor of temperament or of upbringing which makes for greater or less effective intelligence at any time, depending on whether it is directed outward.

Available intelligence tests vary enormously in the degree to which they satisfy the ideal requirements of test construction. The common justification of such tests may be summarized : (*a*) there is one objective standard of marking for every one; (*b*) the influence of chance prejudices is greatly reduced; (*c*) the tests have (or ought to have) been tried out on a fully representative sample of those for whom they are intended, so that we know what performance can reasonably be expected of children of the ages concerned; (*d*) in the case of the better tests, we know how the tests are correlated with other measures such as school examination results, heights and weights, parental occupations, family sizes, etc. Since these ideals are often imperfectly realized, the following questionnaire should perhaps be completed before deciding how much trust to place in any given test :

(1) Name of the test? Is it an individual or a group test?
(2) Name and profession of the maker?
(3) Chronological ages for which it is suitable?
(4) Educational ages for which it is suitable?
(5) Number of children on which the test is standardized? Their educational categories? The districts to which they belong?
(6) Coefficient of reliability or consistency? And its method of calculation?
(7) Coefficients of validity? Found by correlating the test's results with which other assessments?
(8) Cost of using the test? And are there any restrictions on its use?

Origins of Intelligence. One aim of intelligence tests has been to measure inborn intellectual capacity. It is well recognized that this aim is not completely or directly achieved. Results are influenced in varying degrees by environmental circumstances such as home background, education, emotional security, or specific practice or coaching. Many inquiries into such influences were brought together in the twenty-seventh Year-Book of the American National Society for the Study of Education (1928). Barbara Burks suggested that, of the total variation or variance of intelligence test scores, 17 per cent. was due to home influences, while 75 per cent. was due to innate and heritable factors. The maximum contribution of good home conditions was 20 points of I.Q., but this was unusual. Gertrude Hildreth and Florence Goodenough reported that neither favourable school environment nor the experience of nursery training had much effect on Binet intelligence test scores. Heilman thought that 50 per cent. of the variance could be explained by hereditary factors, and attributed less than 13 per cent. and 1 per cent. respectively to school and home. Jones and Ruch found that students who had low intelligence scores were not generally able to compensate for this by hard work. Hoefer and Hardy found a slight connection between physical improvement and improved intelligence score. Kathleen Greene found that two hours' coaching could leave considerable effects even after a year. These findings are interesting but inconclusive. In each case, so much depends on the details of the experiment. Study of the details makes the experiments clearer. But then the various experiments tend to prove less comparable than at first sight.

In recent publications in this country various discussions of environmental influences have appeared. Burt (1955) concludes that "at least 75 per cent. of the measurable variance (based on carefully checked assessments) is attributable to differences in genetic constitution, and less than 25 per cent. to environmental conditions." C. W. Valentine (1956), considering the narrow question of how much intelligence scores are improved by practice, compares the results obtained by 921 boys who did two Moray House group tests of intelligence, with an interval of a week or so between the two. Of these, 172 boys obtained precisely the same score on both occasions. The average fluctuation for the whole group was 4 points. Peel (1953) found that practice caused an average improvement of 6 points over a period of two months, and of 3.5 points over six months. Summarizing one coaching experiment, Alfred Yates (1953) reports that, "in a large-scale inquiry involving twenty junior schools, the coached children made a mean gain of approximately 5 points, the children who were given unassisted practice showed a mean gain of 6 points, and the control group's gain was between 2 and 3 points." He concludes that coaching is unnecessary and undesirable. Instead, practice tests should be used shortly before any real test. Others have reported larger gains as a result of coaching. Some evidence has been put forward that different kinds of schooling may be associated with a rise or fall in the average I.Q.

The association of the I.Q. with socio-economic conditions has been established, but this does not tell us how much is due to the conditions themselves and how much to inherited factors. The accompanying table (Fig. 2) from *Social Implications of the 1947 Scottish Mental Survey* shows how the highest occupational class has the largest *proportion* of high scorers; but the fifth occupational class —skilled manual workers—has the largest absolute number of high scorers on the intelligence test.

It can be seen that the evidence about hereditary and environmental influences on intelligence is indirect. The teacher must recognize this, but remember that his prime concern is to harness the favourable environmental factors as best he can.

Gifted Children. A most thorough study of the

Occupational Class	Thirty-six day Sample N_1	Scoring Sixty and More N_2	N_2 as Percentage of 416	N_2 as Percentage of N_1
I	221	66	15.8	29.9
2	330	33	7.9	10.0
3	236	44	10.6	18.6
4	556	63	15.1	11.3
5	2392	133	31.9	5.6
6	1190	31	7.5	2.6
7	1132	24	5.8	2.1
8	142	8	1.9	5.6
9	428	14	3.4	3.3
Total	6627	416	99.9	6.3

Fig. 2.   Distribution of Occupational Class for Children scoring Sixty or more in the Test (Max. Score = 76)[1]

development of about 1500 gifted children was begun in California in 1921. Lewis Terman and his associates have followed this group of children up to the present time, and it is intended to continue the study in the future. In making the first selection of the gifted children Terman found that the youngest members of school classes were particularly likely to be bright, although their teachers often overlooked this. Most of the experimental group had I.Q.'s over 140. Information was collected about home and school backgrounds and about the children's interests. Anthropometrical measurements and medical assessments were made. The chronological ages of the pre-high-school children ranged from 3 to 13 (average 9.7 years), and the chronological ages of the high-school children from 11 to 19

[1] From *Social Implications of the 1947 Scottish Mental Survey*, by permission of the Scottish Council for Research in Education and the University of London Press, Ltd.

(average 15.2). The occupational classification of the children's fathers is shown in the accompanying table (Fig. 3).

1. Professional   31.4 per cent.
2. Semi-professional and business   50.0
3. Skilled work   11.8
4. Semi-skilled and unskilled work   6.8

Fig. 3. OCCUPATIONAL CLASSIFICATION OF FATHERS OF TERMAN'S GIFTED CHILDREN[1]

Socially and culturally these gifted children were favoured. In height, weight, muscular strength, and other similar measurements the gifted children were slightly superior to other children. Teachers reported 20 per cent. fewer cases of nervousness among the gifted children than among a control group of ordinary children. Medical examination showed the gifted children to be as healthy as, or healthier than, other children. The gifted children tended to advance more quickly through school, and were capable of still more advanced work in some subjects, such as reading and arithmetical reasoning.

A follow-up study of the group six years later, in 1927–28, showed that they maintained their general characteristics, but that there was then more variability within each characteristic. Other studies of the group were initiated in 1936, 1940, and 1945. Eight times as many of the gifted men entered professional or higher business occupations as among Californian men in general. The gifted men experienced very little unemployment—less than ordinary college graduates. Within the gifted group, those men in the first three occupational categories averaged about 6 points higher on the original Binet I.Q.'s than

[1] Based on information from *The Gifted Child Grows Up*, by L. Terman and M. H. Oden (Stanford University Press, 1947).

those in lower occupational groups. "The most notable thing about women's occupations was the relative infrequency with which education was the chosen field." The main interests of the gifted men were sports, photography, and music; of the women, sports, music, and gardening. The most popular magazines were *Time*, *Reader's Digest*, and *Life*. By 1945 about 84 per cent. of both men and women were or had been married. The percentage of the men divorced or separated was 14.4, and of the women, 16.3. The Stanford-Binet test was given to 384 offspring of the gifted; they had a mean I.Q. of 127. This illustrates Galton's law of regression, which asserts that the abilities of children tend to be closer to the average than the abilities of their parents. Very bright parents tend to have slightly less bright children. Dull parents tend to have slightly less dull children. Despite this tendency, there were about twenty-eight times as many of the gifted offspring with I.Q.'s over 150 as one would find in an unselected group of children.

Three persons made independent assessments of 730 gifted men aged 25 or older, to determine the general success with which they had used their superior intellectual ability up to the year 1940. These ratings were used to divide the men into three groups, group A containing the highest fifth, group B the middle 60 per cent., and group C the bottom fifth. Groups A and C were then compared with reference to various specific factors. This comparison indicated that group A included twice as many college graduates and eight times as many professional men, more married men and fewer divorcees. The A's earned two and half times as much, were more often married to college graduates, had wider interests, were more confident and persevering, and more successful in all-round social adjustment. There appeared to be some foundation in childhood for these later discrepancies. The C's, even as children, had shown inferior emotional stability and social adjustments.

Terman considers the question of why his gifted group has thrown up no Goethe, Newton, or Darwin. He suggests that his sample is too small and that "science and scholarship are growing so highly specialized that eminence is becoming progressively more difficult to attain." He adds that the achievement of success through personal contentment is not susceptible of measurement, although the criterion of personal happiness may be as important as that of vocational and material success.

Mental Deficiency. As Terman's study throws much light upon the significance of intelligence in its higher reaches, so the study of mental deficiency brings out the significance of gross defect in intelligence. As brilliancy and deficiency merge slowly into normality at their respective ends of the scale, each has at least an indirect bearing upon our understanding of the nature of intelligent behaviour. The English Mental Deficiency Act of 1927 defined mental deficiency as "a condition of arrested or incomplete development of mind existing before the age of 18 years, whether arising from inherent causes or induced by disease or injury." The Wood report of 1929 advocated the definition of a mental defective as "one who by reason of incomplete mental development is incapable of independent social adaptation." The 1927 Act also defines several categories within the general concept of mental defect:

IDIOTS are "persons in whose case there exists mental defectiveness of such a degree that they are unable to guard themselves against common physical dangers."

IMBECILES are "persons in whose case there exists mental defectiveness, which, though not amounting to idiocy, is yet so pronounced that they are incapable of managing themselves or their affairs, or, in the case of children, of being taught to do so."

THE FEEBLE-MINDED are "persons in whose case there

exists mental defectiveness, which, though not amounting to imbecility, is yet so pronounced that they require care, supervision, and control for their own protection or for the protection of others, or, in the case of children, that they appear to be permanently incapable by reason of such defectiveness of receiving proper benefit from the instruction in ordinary schools."

MORAL DEFECTIVES are "persons in whose case there exists mental defectiveness coupled with strongly vicious or criminal propensities, and who require care, supervision, and control for the protection of others."

One can see that the legal and medical criteria are social and educational rather than purely intellectual. The fourth category is not well founded psychologically and is not used much. The approximate ranges of I.Q. associated with different degrees of mental defect have already been given. For adults one can express the categories in mental ages. An adult idiot has a mental age of less than 2. This means that he needs all the attentions that a baby needs, but has no hope of developing as a normal baby does. For those who look after him he has the disadvantages but not the attractiveness of babyhood. An adult imbecile has a mental age of 3 to 6. He may be able to do more routine things for himself than the idiot. Penrose (1949) thinks that imbeciles can look after themselves to some extent in a sheltered environment which need not be a mental hospital. The adult feeble-minded has a mental age of 7 to 10. He is of very limited capacity and may use what capacity he has in an irresponsible fashion. The higher grades of feeble-minded may be capable of receiving some simple schooling.

According to the 1933 Scottish Mental Survey, the proportion of mentally defective children seemed to be between 1.5 and 3 or 4 per cent. The 1927 English survey by Dr E. O. Lewis indicated an average incidence of

8.6 mental defectives per 1000 of the population. This is the same proportion as that of American Army recruits during the First World War who were found to have mental ages of 8 years or less. Lewis found the highest incidence during the school ages 5 to 19. He further analysed his mental defective sample into 5 per cent. idiots, 20 per cent. imbeciles, and 75 per cent. feeble-minded. The male-female ratio was 9.21 to 7.97. There are more males at the bottom end of the intellectual scale, just as there are at the top. It was common for families to have more than one defective in their midst. Of 966 defectives in one area, sibling groups made up one-third of the total.

Tredgold estimated that mental deficiency had a hereditary basis in 80 per cent. of cases, and that only in 20 per cent. was it mainly environmental. Penrose (1949) has argued more carefully that we cannot make such bold attributions to heredity or environment. The mentally defective are physically inferior to the rest of the population, and there are some diseases which are known to attack the central nervous system and produce mental defect. Gross physical abnormalities are common in lower-grade defectives, but these may be caused by conditions other than mental defect. In the Colchester Survey (1938) of 1280 patients 24 per cent. showed no definite clinical abnormalities. Penrose suggests that at the border-line of feeble-mindedness intellectual defect by itself is rarely enough to require certification. Certification is made necessary by additional factors : "The idiots need attention on account of their helplessness and the feeble-minded need supervision on account of their propensities for maladjustment in the community."

Defectives "are naturally very friendly and are particularly susceptible to influence during the formative years." About half of all feeble-minded children have speech defects and can benefit from opportunities to sing, act in plays, and recite. Games, sports, and club activities, such as Scouting and Guiding, are advocated. Where drawing, painting, and similar activities are enjoyed they should be encouraged.

Mental defect should be distinguished from mental disorder or mental illness. Mental defect is what has been discussed in the previous paragraphs. Mental disorder is a temperamental or personality upset which may have been precipitated by environmental stresses and strains, and which may vent itself in various abnormal states, such as excessive anxiety or aggressiveness, or delusions, or certain physical states. Mental disorders do occur in a proportion of those who are mentally defective and make treatment all the more difficult, but for the present purpose mental disorders will be discussed separately in another chapter.

Burt (1937) calculated that the proportion of educable mental defectives in London was 1.5 per cent. of the total age group, and in a rural area 3 per cent. of the age group. In his study of general educational backwardness he concluded that innate, intellectual dullness was the commonest cause. In his study of delinquent children, intellectual disabilities were only the fifth cause in order of importance, although they occurred in four times as many delinquents as in a comparable group of non-delinquents. Teachers who have to deal with children in schools for the educationally sub-normal, or with the dull children in the 70 to 85 range of I.Q. in ordinary schools, have a special service to perform for the community and for the children in their charge, if they can bring out the best in these duller children without worrying too much about conventional scholastic standards. This does not mean doing anything in a slovenly fashion, but doing simple things well. It means emphasizing the practical and personal side of things. It is a job requiring patience, and it might be good policy to limit the period of time devoted to it in the professional life of any one teacher, unless he or she was particularly absorbed in the work.

Practical Conclusions. The general discussion of intelligence in this chapter suggests several practical conclusions for the teacher. Firstly, intelligence should be distinguished from docility in the classroom. Intelligence should, admittedly, enable a person to learn better, but an impression of greater intelligence than actually exists may occasionally be given by quiet behaviour, by assiduity, or by being older than other pupils in the class. This does not matter provided that the achievements based on these characteristics are not expected to persist when intrinsically much more difficult tasks are presented at the secondary school or at college.

Secondly, the imperfections of intelligence testing should not obscure the relatively high accuracy of the best tests in showing a person's general intellectual level and promise. The I.Q., for example, is usually found to be the best *single* predictor of academic success, and is closely associated with success in jobs which are generally admitted to require intelligence. Although a person's I.Q. may be expected to vary slightly, a difference of 5 points is not of great importance. Certain *possible* border-lines, such as 70 I.Q. for entry to an E.S.N. school or 115 I.Q. for grammar-school entry, are useful and justified in practice. Everyone knows that other factors are and must be taken into account, but there is no escaping the primacy and extent of the importance of general intellectual ability, whether one is catering for those who demonstrate a high or a low degree of it.

Thirdly, when accurate assessments of intelligence have been used for educational or vocational guidance, so that each individual attempts the general level of work of which he seems capable, the teacher must then enable each to achieve as much as possible at his own level. We might say paradoxically that the teacher must both remember and forget the intellectual limits of his pupils.

Fourthly, children between 7 and 10 who have I.Q.'s between 50 and 70 or 75, and who are bound to be backward educationally, should be admitted to schools for educationally sub-normal children soon enough to let them benefit from such special educational treatment. The mental ages of children in an E.S.N. primary department range from about $2\frac{1}{2}$ to $8\frac{1}{2}$. Lloyd (1953) and Cleugh (1957) agree that, while E.S.N. schools are few in number, they should not be used by backward children who are in the dull range of intelligence (70–80 I.Q.), nor by backward children who are maladjusted and happen to be a nuisance in ordinary schools. To apply this suggested policy successfully, the ascertainment of possible E.S.N. children should be done systematically by the education authority. Education in the E.S.N. school has to be primarily social and moral. Lloyd suggests that only one in five E.S.N. children may be ready to start formal reading before entering a secondary department. She says of teaching E.S.N. children that "they need more direction and supervision and more external stimuli—they must be encouraged, or even forced, to engage in purposeful activities, rather than be left free to bypass these in favour of effortless occupations."

The existence of 8 to 10 per cent. of children in the dull and backward category means that ordinary schools must try to make regular provision for slow learners. Cleugh suggests that, in a school for 500 pupils, four teachers should cater for the backward, although at the start only one of the four might have special interests and qualifications in this field. The other three might divide their efforts between backward and other children.

Fifthly, the account of Terman's study of gifted children reminds the teacher of their much wider capacities at every stage. This suggests that the teacher must provide materials, books, experiences, and exercises to occupy them. If he must simplify and go slow for the dull child he must also enrich the school's offering to the bright child. It is too easy to let him waste his time in trifling or in doing the teacher's odd jobs when he should be meeting some more challenging task. In the secondary school it does not seem justifiable to hinder the academic progress of the very bright child just because most children are slower. Education according to age, ability, and aptitude is the right of the bright child as well as of other children.

Chapter Five

Educational Assessments

THOSE taking part in any human enterprise have a natural desire to know how they are getting on at each stage: the supervisors have to know so that they can plan the details of the next stage; the other participants want to know so that they have a sense of achievement and purpose to keep them going. The importance of this has long been recognized by educators, and the problem is how to make the best possible educational assessments. The aim of this chapter is to present some of the most general ideas of statistical method, so that those who have no need or desire to go deeper into the subject may still have that rudimentary grasp of principle which is indispensable for the appreciation of much educational practice. Without understanding fully the intricacies of computation and advanced statistical method, any teacher can still develop some idea of the technical problems of assessing people.

Many studies have been made of the effectiveness of traditional examinations and interviews. Ballard (1923) campaigned for the new 'objective' tests, and related the story of the Columbia University history professor who wrote a set of model answers to help himself in marking an examination. The answers accidentally fell into the hands of his colleagues on the examining board and received marks from 40 to 80 per cent., the pass mark being 60! Valentine (1932) criticized traditional examinations for the strain they created, for their perversion of true education, and for the chance variability that entered into the questions set and into the standards of marking. Hartog and Rhodes (1936) described in detail some careful studies of how marks may vary from one examiner to the next, or even from one occasion to the next with the same examiner and the same scripts. These studies show that much variability is to be found in the marking of Honours scripts in mathematics and history, and in interviewing by experienced interviewers, as well as in awarding school certificate marks. In slight mitigation of these findings, part of the variation is due to genuine differences in examiners' beliefs about what matters, or even to short-term changes in such beliefs. Secondly, when a population is already highly selected (grammar-school pupils, university students, Civil Service interviewees) there may be relatively small differences within the groups concerned. As the selectors are concerned to find what differences there are, they may sometimes impose artificial distinctions upon the groups.

Describing Groups Statistically. Individuals cannot be assessed in a vacuum. They are assessed in relation to appropriate groups—an eight-year-old in relation to what is expected of eight-year-olds, a handicapped child in relation to similarly handicapped children, and so on. This does not mean that all the members of a group can be treated in the same way, but only that there must be some scale of reference if they are to be assessed at all. In establishing such a scale two factors must always be considered—the central tendency and the range of the group. These can be illustrated in terms of teachers' marks. One teacher will take an optimistic view and award marks to a class in such a way that the class average is 60 per cent. A harder judge will award marks which average only 50 per cent. But even if teachers achieve the same class average they may do so in very different ways. Teacher 'A' marks half a dozen compositions 45, 53, 56, 62, 67, and 77. Teacher 'B' marks them 55, 57, 59, 61, 63, 65. Teacher 'C' marks them 45, 45, 45, 70, 75, 80. They all average 60, but the spread or scatter of scores differs in each case.

Scores	Difference from Group Average	Difference Squared
80	20	400
75	15	225
70	10	100
45	−15	225
45	−15	225
45	−15	225
360		1400

$$Average = \ 360 \div 6 = 60$$
$$Variance = 1400 \div 6 = 233.3$$
$$Standard\ Deviation\ (\sigma) = \sqrt{233.3} \quad = 15.27$$

Fig. 4.   CALCULATING THE VARIANCE

The two common statistics used to describe a group in summary fashion are the *mean* and the *variance*. The mean, or average, is simply the total of the scores divided by the number of people who make them. The variance is a mathematical expression of the extent to which the individuals in a group deviate from the average of the group. Often the spread of scores is expressed as a *standard deviation*. This is the square root of the variance. If a set of scores had a mean of 60 and a standard deviation of 10 we could speak of the score 70 as being one standard deviation (1σ) above the mean, or of 45 as being one and a half standard deviations below the mean $(-1\frac{1}{2}\sigma)$. The standard deviations of the marks allotted by teachers A, B, and C in the preceding paragraph are (to the nearest whole numbers) 10, 3, and 15. Without this precise measure of the different degrees to which the teachers have spread their marks, we might believe that a mark of 70 was the same whoever awarded it. In fact, teacher A's 70 corresponds to teacher B's 63, and each of these to teacher C's 75.

Instead of the mean score, the *median* may be calculated. The median may be preferable if there are only a few cases, or if there is a preponderance of high or of low scores. The median is the score of the middle person when the scores are listed from highest to lowest. With the six compositions mentioned above where the number of scores is even, the median is taken to be midway between the third and fourth scores. The three teachers have medians of 59, 60, and 57.5.

These common statistics have many uses. This can be illustrated by turning again to the problem of making assessments comparable. Three main devices are used. Firstly, markers decide exactly what they are trying to assess and compile detailed instructions about the marking scheme. For example, they may decide that their marks must approximate to a given average and to a certain degree of scatter. This prevents an individual examiner from imposing his own arbitrary standards on the group, but leaves him free to make his personal discriminations among individuals within the group and within the fixed scale of marking. Secondly, the employment of more than one assessor and more than one kind of examination or test may help to cancel out the bias of single assessments. Thirdly, if assessments vary to any extent it may be possible to *scale* them.

Scaling. Children in different schools might be assessed by their headmasters in respect of ability in English. How are ratings from different schools to be made comparable? If all the children in all the schools do an English test which is marked as objectively as possible in accordance with a scale of known mean and variance, then the test scores can be used to bring the headmasters' ratings on to the same scale. The order of merit of pupils in any school is unchanged, but variations arising from different school standards are partly eliminated. The conscientious marker is liable to protest that when he gives Johnny no marks he does not expect to find the 0 scaled up to 20, and Jimmy's well-earned 90 reduced to 80. From an adult point of view it does not really matter whether the poorest performer is labelled 0 or 20, but the performer himself may mistakenly feel that he has genuinely improved as a result of this wonderful statistical trick.

Let us suppose that the headmaster's assessments in one school have a mean of 55 and a standard deviation of 9. A child marked 64 by the headmaster is one standard deviation above the headmaster's mean $(55+9)$. Let us also suppose that the objective test used to standardize the results from several schools has a mean of 100 and a standard deviation of 15. On the new scale, the child's score will be one new standard deviation (15) above the new mean (100)—that is, 115. The formula for this transformation is:

$$\text{new mark} = \text{new mean} + \left(\frac{\text{new standard deviation}}{\text{old standard deviation}} \times \begin{array}{l}\text{difference}\\\text{between old}\\\text{mark and}\\\text{old mean}\end{array} \right)$$

To give one more example, suppose that the old mark was 61. Then,

$$\text{new mark} = 100 + \left(\frac{15}{9} \times (61-55) \right)$$
$$= 110$$

The numerical examples of means, medians, standard deviations, and scaling that have been given in this chapter illustrate only the general nature of the various calculations. In practice a greater variety of computing methods is used.

Intelligence Quotients.   The use of standardized tests has been mentioned. One of the best-known types of such a test is that which gives us intelligence quotients. Intelligence quotients can be arrived at by two different routes. The first way is based on the idea that children at different ages manifest intelligence by being able to do different things. An average seven-year-old may be expected, among other things, to show that he understands a simple pictorial absurdity. A ten-year-old may be expected to repeat correctly a series of six digits in at least one trial out of three. If a child can solve a series of problems that add up to what might be expected of an average ten-year-old we say that the child has a *mental age* of 10. If the child's ordinary or chronological age is also 10 we calculate his I.Q. as being

$$\frac{\text{mental age}}{\text{chronological age}} \times 100$$

$$i.e., \frac{10}{10} \times 100$$

$$i.e., 100$$

But the child of 10 might succeed in a sample of problems that was up to the average performance of a twelve-year-old. His I.Q. would then be

$$\frac{12}{10} \times 100 \text{---} i.e., 120.$$

This way of reckoning the I.Q. is not very appropriate after the age of 16, and even before that age is not necessarily the best estimate of the I.Q.

In the second method a large number of items are tried out on a group comparable to that for which the test is designed. Those items that everybody passes are of little use, for they do not distinguish among individuals. Those that nobody passes are useless in a similar way. Items of intermediate difficulty will be suitable for different parts of the test. The easier items, passed by a large proportion, can go at the beginning, the difficult items at the end of the test. When suitable items have been put in the appropriate order the whole test is administered to a representative sample of those for whom it is ultimately intended. The scores are scaled so that they have a predetermined mean and standard deviation. The mean is commonly 100 and the standard deviation 15. This transformation of the scores actually obtained on to a standardized scale does not alter the shape of the distribution. With an intelligence test made in this fashion, I.Q. means the performance of an individual on the test, measured by comparison with the performance of a representative sample of individuals in the same age-range. It is not entirely different from the first type of I.Q., but it omits the idea of mental age. Nor is it entirely different from the assessments of common-sense. Like them, it works by comparing an individual with some group, but, unlike most of them, it is based on a carefully defined *representative* group. This does not mean that the groups used for standardizing a test are perfectly representative. There are always margins of error. But the test-constructor takes more pains (or should) to approximate to the ideal.

Normal Distribution.   The type of distribution of scores given by a test depends on its purpose. Tests can be made to give any desired distribution. One of the commonest forms of distribution in use is the *normal distribution*. While the normal distribution of height is an observed fact, intelligence quotients are normally distributed partly because of the way the tests are made. This is not an entirely arbitrary convenience, for, as has been suggested before, common experience suggests that it is easier to discriminate between those who possess or lack a quality in a marked degree than between those who seem to have it in an ordinary degree. Test-constructors favour this view when they select a test item partly on the grounds that it discriminates well between those whose total scores put them in the top third and those whose total scores put them in the bottom third of the whole group. The accompanying diagram (Fig. 5) shows the appearance of a normal distribution of scores, and the proportion of the group in different parts of the distribution.

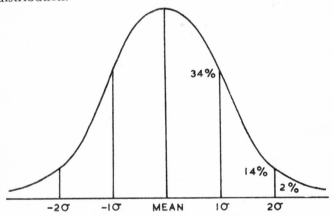

Fig. 5. NORMAL DISTRIBUTION CURVE

Attainments. Attainments too can be estimated on a standardized scale. A *reading age* or an *arithmetic age* of 10, for example, indicates the performances that are known to be typical of children at this age. A general *educational age* would be based on averaging reading age, arithmetic age, etc. Each of these can be expressed as a quotient by dividing by chronological age and multiplying by 100.

Johnny's chronological age is   10

His mental age is   12

His intelligence quotient is $\dfrac{12}{10} \times 100 = 120$

His reading age is   10

His reading quotient is $\dfrac{\text{reading age}}{\text{chronological age}} \times 100$

$$= \dfrac{10}{10} \times 100 = 100$$

His arithmetic age is   11

His arithmetic quotient is $\dfrac{\text{arithmetic age}}{\text{chronological age}} \times 100$

$$= \dfrac{11}{10} \times 100 = 110$$

His educational age is $\dfrac{\text{reading age} + \text{arithmetic age}}{2}$

$$= \dfrac{10 + 11}{2} = 10\tfrac{1}{2}$$

His educational quotient is $\dfrac{\text{educational age}}{\text{chronological age}} \times 100$

$$= \dfrac{10\tfrac{1}{2}}{10} \times 100 = 105$$

In summary, Johnny is a boy of 10 with the general intellectual capacity of a boy two years older. His reading ability is just average and his arithmetic is a year in advance of the standard for his age. Neither reading nor arithmetic comes up to his estimated intellectual capacity. It is convenient to use the word 'retarded' when attainments do not come up to mental age, and to use the word 'backward' only when achievements do not come up to chronological age. In ordinary usage, however, teachers do not apply 'retarded' to a bright child, even if he does fall short of his potentialities. The whole system of ages and quotients can be most convenient for the purpose of summarizing certain facts and relationships. Being summaries, they tend to make us forget the complexity of the observations on which they are based. It is easy enough to speak about 'reading age,' but reading is a complex skill ranging from the ability to read out individual words from a list to the ability to understand instructions or explanations about intrinsically complex matters.

What has been said hitherto illustrates one of the main purposes of statistics—namely, to summarize the characteristics of groups of people, and thus give points of reference for judging individuals in the groups. Statistics serve another major purpose: they help us to measure the relationships between groups, with respect to different characteristics such as intelligence or educational attainments.

Correlation. Correlation is the calculation of how closely two groups resemble one another in respect of some characteristic. The numerical values of a correlation coefficient (r) range from — 1 through 0 to + 1. A value of — 1 means that two qualities are in an inverse, or upside-down, relationship to one another. The better you are on X, always the worse you are on Y. A value of + 1 means a perfect correspondence. Your places on X and Y are identical, whether high or low. A correlation of 0 means there is absolutely no relationship between X and Y, either one way or the other. It is more usual to find intermediate values for the coefficients, and there is a tendency for desirable, and undesirable, psychological qualities to be positively correlated. Able people tend to be capable of succeeding in many things, and dull people tend to be dull at most things.

Some may think of correlation as a purely statistical device. But, in a less precise way, we make such comparisons all the time in daily life. We want to know what places are correlated with having a good holiday, in what shops good clothes are correlated with moderate prices, what kinds of men and women are correlated with our own prospects of agreeable husbands or wives, what manners and fashions are correlated with being acceptable to our neighbours, and so in a hundred other cases. Teachers may have a special interest in knowing how far success in arithmetic and other aspects of mathematics is correlated with success in English and languages, or success in primary school with secondary-school success.

The accompanying correlation table (Fig. 6) shows the appearance of this most useful kind of chart. The example shows how the intelligence test scores of 152 first-year university students compare with their average degree examination marks for the four subjects physics, chemistry, botany, and zoology. The numerical value of the correlation is +0.6. This indicates a considerable measure of agreement, especially in such a highly selected group of people. The tendency is for those who are bright as indicated by the intelligence test to be bright as indicated by the university results. There are individual exceptions to this rule. About one-sixth of the students are above average on the intelligence test and yet below average in the university examinations. Another sixth are discrepant in the opposite direction, gaining above-average marks in their examinations and below-average scores on the intelligence test.

Given a persistent correlation of +0.6 between intelligence scores and the university marks, the intelligence scores would enable one to predict the university results

Intelligence Scores	Average Marks for Four University Subjects								Total No. of Students
	40 44	45 49	50 54	55 59	60 64	65 69	70 74	75 79	
90–94			2		1				3
85–89			3	4	2	3			12
80–84		1	5	6	4		1	1	18
75–79	3		3	3	4	3	1		17
70–74	1	2	3	3	7	4	3		23
65–69	2	2	6	6	3	4	2		25
60–64	1	1	1	3	3	3	1		13
55–59	2	1	4	3	5	2			17
50–54	2	1	3	1					7
45–49	2	3	3	2					10
40–44	3	1							4
35–39	1			2					3
Total No. of Students	17	12	33	33	29	19	8	1	152

$$r = +0.6$$

Fig. 6. CORRELATION OF INTELLIGENCE TEST SCORES
AND UNIVERSITY MARKS

20 per cent. better than by guessing. The correlation has to be higher than $+0.8$ in order to achieve a 50 to 100 per cent. improvement over guess-work prediction.

Suppose that the universities contemplated using the intelligence test to select students in future years, would the evidence of this correlation chart help them? If it were insisted that every candidate for admission should have an intelligence score over 50, then according to the above chart those shut out would include 10 failures and 7 who would reach the university pass-mark of 50. While those with the very highest intelligence score include no university failures, those with the lowest do include university 'passes'—testimony, no doubt, to hard work and dogged intention. Moreover, a sound decision would require the comparison of the intelligence scores with other examination results, and in respect of other groups of students. Even then there would be problems left over. Sixth-form teachers might coach their students for the university entrance test, just as many eleven-year-olds have been coached in the intelligence tests used as part of the procedure for allocating children to secondary schools.

Some Advanced Aspects of Assessment

Analysing Factors. If a group of children has done a number of tests all the results can be correlated. If the correlations between pairs of tests are high this suggests that the tests may be measuring the same things. By performing certain arithmetical operations with the correlation coefficients it is possible to show that there is a *limited* number of factors in the test performances. For example, although there were four tests, the analysis of their intercorrelations might suggest that only two separate qualities were being measured : factor A might run through tests 1, 2, and 3 (they might all be arithmetical in nature); factor S might run through tests 1, 3, and 4 (they might all include spatial problems). A *general* factor is one that is present in all the tests. A *group* factor is one that is present in only one group of the tests. A *specific* factor is limited to a single test.

Four fundamental factors have been suggested by educational researches. They are :

(1) general mental ability (g);
(2) verbal, numerical, and educational ability (v : ed);

(3) practical, mechanical, spatial, and physical ability (k : m);

(4) perseverance or conscientiousness (X).

These are not entirely distinct from one another, but they suggest four useful areas of assessment to which a teacher may give attention.

Good Sampling. One of the first questions to be asked about any evidence is whether it is based on an adequate sample of the people concerned. The special pleading of everyday conversation, where wide generalizations may be drawn from a few atypical cases, is a good example of how the need for an adequate sample is ignored. In calculating any of the usual statistics this potential defect in sampling is anticipated by calculating its *standard error.* This is a measure of how much the primary statistic might vary were we to repeat the experiment or observation with a different sample of the same population. If the indication is that the variation might be large, then the original statistic can hardly provide the basis for a generalization.

In this matter of sampling there is a very common confusion between a *random* sample and a *representative* sample. People often speak about the former when they mean the latter. A random sample must be chosen in such a way that human bias can have no influence. This is properly achieved by the technical device of using a table of random numbers. A representative sample, which is what most non-specialists think of, can be chosen so as to represent sub-groups according to their actual proportions in the total population under study.

Reliability, Validity, Significance, and Objectivity. A second important question is whether certain words commonly used in describing educational researches are being used in their technical senses or in a wider sense. The point can be illustrated by referring to four of the commonest of such expressions. 'Reliable,' 'valid,' 'significant,' and 'objective,' have special meanings when used with statistical reference. Every observation is liable to error in some degree. Every possibility of error cannot be excluded, but the likely magnitude of variation due to error can be estimated. The *reliability coefficient* of a test is an estimate of how much test results may vary from one occasion to another, given the same test and the same people doing it. The people on the second occasion may, of course, have improved in virtue of their experience on the first. There are devices for getting round this difficulty, but we need not concern ourselves with them here. Statistical reliability is, in a sense, the extent to which the test correlates with itself on different occasions. A good test should have a reliability coefficient of at least $+0.9$. Otherwise a single person's score may differ from one occasion to the next, not because the person has changed, but because of some defect in the test.

The *validity coefficient* of a test is an estimate of how well a test measures what it is supposed to measure. Such a coefficient can be obtained by correlating the test results with some other criterion of the quality measured. Intelligence as indicated by I.Q.'s at the age of 11 could be compared with intelligence as assessed by school examination results at 16 or 17. The correlation of $+0.6$, already quoted, between intelligence scores and university marks could be considered a validity coefficient, although a rather poor one both in respect of its size and of the short time of nine months elapsing between the test and the examinations. A validity coefficient does not by itself make a test valid in the non-technical sense of 'trustworthy,' 'working properly,' 'all in order.' But a series of validity coefficients, showing that different assessments correlate with one another, makes it increasingly plausible to assume that there is some central factor or characteristic which does genuinely exist.

'Significant' is a word used in the vaguest way on many occasions. Particularly, people are apt to use it without telling us what is signified. It was long popular to say that art was 'significant form.' While this carries a suggestion of some worth-while idea, it is almost too general to be useful. Statistical significance simply means that some relationship is genuinely based on the factors being studied and not on chance. A correlation of $+0.15$ may be statistically significant but have no other useful significance. Since the correlation is statistically significant, it does genuinely hold between the two variables under study, but it would not give us much help in predicting one from a knowledge of the other.

'Objectivity' is another much-abused word. In educational measurement a test is objective in so far as its results are independent of variations in human judgment. Variations in interpreting the problems are limited by a short, simple formulation of them, and by offering perhaps only five solutions, of which the correct one is to be underlined. This has the disadvantage for the tester and tested that they tend to exclude from consideration problems and solutions that are intricate, subtle, and novel—in fact, the very things that matter to an intelligent person. Variations in marking the tests are similarly limited by marking keys and detailed instructions. The 'objectivity' obtained at this price is justified only by the need to assess large numbers quickly and reasonably fairly.

Statistical inquiry has much to live down. "You can prove anything by statistics." "Statistics prove nothing." "Lies, damned lies, and statistics." But the problems of statistics are partly the problems of common sense and are unavoidable in making educational assessments.

Chapter Six

Educational Backwardness

EDUCATIONAL and psychological principles are most severely tested when something goes wrong. If the principles are sound they should enable us to diagnose what is wrong and to put it right. The problem of backwardness is a good example, for most teachers are certain to face it, and some to find it in discouragingly persistent and intractable forms. How does the psychology of learning, of intelligence, and of educational assessment help a teacher to deal with this common, practical problem?

It was once possible to 'explain' backwardness as the product of inferior natural capacity, of bone-laziness, or of deliberate resistance to teaching. The child or his parents were at fault, and the teacher was exonerated from any responsibility for finding new ways of progress. Few teachers are now satisfied with such an attitude. The extent to which backwardness can be analysed and remedied is still an open question, but much more can be and is done than in the past.

'Backwardness' is obviously a relative term. A university student who is far from backward in relation to the whole population of young people may be backward in relation to the standards prevailing inside the university. Children with general abilities corresponding to an I.Q. of under 70 are sometimes called 'backward,' although they are technically called 'educationally sub-normal,' or 'mentally defective.' These uses of the word cannot be abolished, but some psychologists and teachers accept a more specific connotation for the word 'backward.' It is applied to children who are not educationally sub-normal in the technical sense, but whose educational attainments lag at least 25 to 20 per cent. behind what is normal for their chronological age. Their attainment quotients are under 85 or 80. If this is the case for all the main school-subjects the child is *generally* backward, if for only one or two subjects he is *specifically* backward. This is a useful and more precise conception of backwardness. At the same time it has to be noted that educational attainments can be measured with only a partial degree of precision, and that different tests are not always comparable. It is hardly worth while knowing that a child has this or that quotient, or this or that degree of backwardness, unless the basis of the figures is given, together with descriptive comments about the quality and circumstances of the child's performance. It is especially dangerous to pin quotients on children during their first two or three years at school. During these years some children are obviously backward in a popular sense, but they must have time to settle down before they are labelled 'backward' in the technical sense.

Some backward children have I.Q.'s between about 70 and 85—that is, in the dull range of intelligence. If other signs of their general ability are consistent with the estimate of the I.Q., then such children are considered dull and backward. Not only do they lag behind normal attainments but they do not give intellectual promise of ever doing anything else. The teacher must lower the academic sights to give these children a chance of doing well what they are able to, so that they do not perform badly by having too much foisted upon them. If their dullness is only temporary they can catch up in the future. Normally this will not be the case, and they deserve suitable material and teaching for the present.

As mentioned in a previous chapter, the word 'retarded'

is used to designate those who are lagging not behind their chronological age but behind their mental age. As with backwardness, it is convenient to decree that the retardation should be at least 15 or 20 per cent. Retardation may exist at any intellectual level. A dull and backward child may also be retarded if his attainments are well below even what a child of his mental age would normally reach. A very bright child may be retarded if, for example, he has a mental age well in advance of his chronological age, but an attainment age only equal to his chronological age. Attainments need not always match mental age. A boy of 10 with a mental age of 13 is still only a boy of 10. He needs an enriched programme at his own ten-year-old level, not the ordinary curriculum for a thirteen-year-old.

Without the advances which have been described in the reliable assessment of general intelligence and specific educational attainments, the concepts of backwardness and retardation would have remained vaguer than they are, and research into causes and treatment would have been hindered by lack of the means to identify the backward and retarded children on a sufficiently large scale. Burt (1937) made an intensive study of general backwardness in 193 boys and 198 girls between the ages of 7 and 14. One of the signal merits of his study is that it included, for purposes of comparison, control groups of 200 boys and 200 girls who matched the backward children in sex, age, and the school attended, but who reached the normal standard in educational attainments and progress. This gives greater significance to the differences between backward and non-backward children.

"The fact of multiple determination" was one of the most prominent in Burt's study. The child's physical conditions were unfavourable in three-quarters of the cases, the temperamental conditions in one-third, and school conditions in one-sixth. On the average there were three sets of unfavourable circumstances contributing to each case of backwardness. The single factor which was most closely associated with backwardness $(r = +0.7)$ was poor general intelligence. This and other findings caused Burt to conclude that "the chief reasons for educational backwardness are psychological." He saw the problem as being social as much as educational. Its solution depended on making the teacher his own psychologist. He did not mean a psychological theorizer, for he describes the ideal teacher of the backward as being

> a bright, adaptable person, physically active and mentally vivacious, firm, patient, sympathetic, and inspired by strong commonsense. . . . He should, in short, be a man of a practical as distinct from an academic turn of mind, with leanings that are concrete rather than bookish, a talent for manual work and expression rather than for what is merely literary or scholastic.

This may be a counsel of perfection, but it is valuable as indicating the attitude that can help the backward.

Schonell (1942) gave his attention to the problems of specific backwardness in reading, spelling, and composition. Of 317 boys and girls between the ages of 7 and 12 in a primary school, 11.4 per cent. were found to be backward in both English and arithmetic. A small extra number were backward in only one of these subjects. The 11.4 per cent. could be divided into 7.2 per cent. who were intellectually dull and 4.2 per cent. who were average or better. Schonell saw backwardness as a problem in individual differences, and pointed to four kinds of difference that have to be taken into account:

(1) Intellectual characteristics.
(2) Emotional tendencies.
(3) Physical conditions.
(4) Environmental influences.

From this framework he developed a diagnostic method of nine stages :

 (1) Measurement of general intelligence.
 (2) Application of scholastic tests.
 (3) Application of diagnostic tests in the backward subject or subjects.
 (4) Application of sensory tests.
 (5) Assessment of emotional characteristics.
 (6) Recording of interests.
 (7) Brief inquiry into personal history.
 (8) Study of educational history in the backward subject.
 (9) Talk with child concerning attitude towards disability and inquiry into possible anxieties or conflicts.[1]

One of the features that struck Schonell most forcibly was how frequently and obviously emotional factors entered into the causation of specific backwardness, tempting him to believe that what the child most needed was a fresh start. In terms of learning theory, a strongly inhibiting negative drive has become attached to the existing learning situation. A change of stimuli is necessary to establish a positive attitude towards learning. The change may be in the method, as when games and activity replace more traditional teaching methods. It may be a new text-book to give the sense of a fresh start. It may be a new and more sympathetic teacher, a change of class, or even a change outside the school to an adjustment centre or child-guidance clinic. Often it will be a change back to an earlier stage in the learning process. A boy may have been plunged into the formal side of learning to read before he had a sufficient background of spoken English or the opportunity to become interested in the talking and story-telling which precede an interest in reading. It may be necessary to go back to this pre-reading stage even if

[1] From *Backwardness in the Basic Subjects* (Oliver and Boyd, 1942), pp. 93-94.

the boy is well past the usual chronological age for it. The teacher who regards this temporary return as wasteful of time, or childish, or frivolous, may labour long in vain to build the advanced edifice on non-existent foundations. In a large class the teacher cannot deal adequately with seriously backward children. They must be given special opportunities in some kind of adjustment or improvement class. But the ordinary class teacher, even in a large class, can refrain from penalizing or deriding a backward child whom he is unable to help in any other way.

The backward child might equally be discussed in terms of *Gestalt* psychology. Learning, school, books, the blackboard, the teacher's desk, the teacher and headmaster, the parents at home, belong in the same pattern with failure, punishment, criticism, scorn, perhaps ultimately neglect. Someone has to destroy this conformation and associate learning and all its trappings with success, reward, approval, consideration, and hope. Hardly anyone would dare to speak to a teacher about his shortcomings in the way in which teachers are free to talk to their pupils. There is a moral here. A teacher might ask, How would the Head or the Director of Education have to approach me in order to enrol my willing co-operation in one of his ventures? or, How did those university or training-college lecturers approach me who made me willingly study their subjects? and then, How must I approach my pupils if I am to win their best efforts? The answer would often be that the leader shows a combination of genuine and infectious interest in his subject, a real command of the subject, a strong desire to communicate the subject to others, and a sincere respect for the principle that, however ardently the leader pleads his cause, the potential learner must be free to make his own choice.

This does not mean, of course, that the teacher will plead with the backward child to take an interest in reading or arithmetic. Reading and arithmetic must be made so interesting that the backward child cannot resist them any more than he can resist an iced lollipop. There are two main barriers to this compelling arousal of interest. Firstly, some teachers have difficulty in persuading themselves to go far enough back in the learning process. They refuse to do six-year-old work with eight-year-olds or ten-year-olds. It has already been granted that in large classes such an argument has considerable force because of practical difficulties. But the only progress in this case is through going back to the point where the backward child can succeed and be commended, and begin to doubt whether learning is all painfulness. Similarly, some are shy of associating themselves with 'unorthodox' devices—special individual books, word games, or any special attention or privilege for the undeserving backward child. Why should the backward have what the ordinary child does not have? The answer is that an inadequate command of the three 'R's' is such a deprivation, from the point of view of a child's esteem as well as of his later practical needs, that any special attention he may receive is a small enough outlay to let him recoup his losses so far as he may. Here are two cardinal principles of learning, assumed by all theorizers, but sometimes ignored in practice. Learning must bring a reward of *some* kind. And any specific piece of learning must be within the capabilities of the learner.

It has been admitted that it is not easy for teachers, hard-pressed by routine work, to apply the principles that are known to be essential for the backward child. How much more difficult is it for them to accept some measure of responsibility for attacking causes of backwardness that lie in the home rather than the school. The teacher cannot change the home, although his standards may percolate via the children. Yet the backwardness, the indiscipline, that manifest themselves in the classroom may be controlled only by influencing the root causes. Parental strife may fill a child with anxieties which paralyse all capacity for work. Late nights may result in sleepy-headedness in school. Lack of concern for schooling, or antipathy to it, in the home may inhibit the child in the school. Ambitious parents may press their child until he rebels even against the learning of which he is capable. Absences from school, associated with some of the above factors or with neurotic illness arising from them, may make the backward child still more backward. When we remember that the backward child is typically handicapped in several ways, and particularly in the most important respect of general intelligence, the difficulty of the problem is clear.

Just because of the difficulty, the teacher must be patient, exercising firmness and fairness, and forgiving many things many times. The worse the child's plight, the more he needs a steady, affectionate, helping interest taken in him by the teacher. Psychological understanding is vital, and such understanding of others depends on first understanding oneself. While the teacher's attitude should be one of patient helpfulness, he must for his own mental health recognize that some backward children have deep-rooted problems which cannot be solved in an ordinary classroom. These cases are serious in more than one sense. They may not improve even in response to the teacher's most enlightened and sympathetic attention, and so cause the teacher to doubt whether such tolerance really pays. This is a delicate psychological situation. It means that the child's anxiety is so strong that he is not ready to give a teacher even the satisfaction of gracefully accepting his goodwill. The child is just like the infant who shouts, "I hate you, Mummy!" although he is really very dependent on Mummy in every sense. If the teacher, or Mummy herself, is too dependent on favourable responses from the child to bolster his or her own sense of security, then the child's apathy or opposition will be received more painfully than it should be. The ability to help the young and dependent springs partly from mature independence in adults.

It is difficult to assess personality reliably in any circumstances, and more so when the picture is obscured by special unknown factors. For the present purpose it may be enough to draw attention to one or two special points. It is unwise to assume too readily that any apparent personality trait is permanent. People do remain the same to a large extent, but they can change, especially if circumstances change markedly. It is also unwise to assume that a trait which appears prominent in one situation will be apparent at all in another. People may be circumspect here but rash there, mild and sociable with their bosom friends but aggressive in some more trying situation. Such divergences could be illustrated without end. And thirdly, it is unwise to assume that aggressive or peaceful behaviour reveals aggressive or peaceful personalities, for either may conceal a personality whose main trait is fear and anxiety. Schonell gives various scales for rating such personality traits as self-confidence, persistence, etc. These are suggestive of worth-while points of inquiry, but the diversity of one person's behaviour militates against any kind of average estimate, even in respect of what seems to be a single quality, such as self-confidence.

An understanding of the emotional basis of backwardness along the lines just suggested is probably the most important step in diagnosis and in remedial work, but it should be associated with our improved understanding of the more mechanical aspects of the learning process. Reading and arithmetic were once taught as if the processes amounted to little more than giving a child of adequate intelligence a passage or a sum of appropriate difficulty. In the case of bright children this view may hold good to some extent. Many educated adults do not recall any particular process of learning to read beyond hearing stories from their mothers and being put in the way of books. The backward child often lacks both the parental stimulus and the intellect which just picks things up. It is all the more essential to know what happens in the process of learning to read or count, so that the slower child can be helped along in correct stages.

Reflection upon the nature of reading and studies of the process of reading have changed aims and methods. Reading aloud was once the main aim, whether or not the material was understood. Now the emphasis is on silent reading to get the meaning of the passage. A logical advance from letters to words to sentences was once the accepted pathway. Now the course leads from what is meaningful to the child (story-telling, associating whole words or sentences with whatever they refer to, making individual reading-books) to reading whole words and sentences, and to the phonic analysis of words as an essential aid to pronouncing new words. Once the child was invited to learn families of words of the 'cat-sat-mat' variety. Now it is appreciated that a child may learn more quickly to distinguish 'cat' and 'hippopotamus' than 'cat' and 'rat.' There is no question of decrying phonic analysis; what matters is that it should serve rather than hinder a satisfying progress in meaningful reading.

Schonell's diagnostic tests are designed not merely to give a child a reading age, but to find just what kind of misunderstandings or gaps exist in his reading knowledge. Does he recognize all the small and capital letters? Does he read in the correct left-to-right direction, or does he reverse words like 'top' or 'tip'? Is his visual discrimination adequate to distinguish 'thread' from 'threab' or 'thred'? Similarly in arithmetic, planned diagnostic tests will indicate not merely how good or how poor a child is (which is probably known already), but precisely which number facts or processes are known or unknown. It is the difference between shaking the machine in the hope that something will make it go, and checking systematically each part of the mechanism to find out which part is defective.

The analogy applies equally to remedial work. Just as the faulty mechanism has to be stripped to the point where things began to go wrong, so the child's learning has to be retraced to the corresponding point. This will usually mean individual teaching in clinics or small classes. Games, practical work, individual reading-books, will help to make the elementary steps successful and palatable for the child whose chronological age may seem to be beyond such 'childish' things. The material has to be sufficiently easy to guarantee success, and yet it must be so designed as not to insult the interests and self-esteem of the older backward child. The longer a backward child is left without remedial teaching, the more awkward does it become to span the gulf between his scholastic needs and his chronological interests.

M. D. Vernon (1957) has provided a valuable critical review of inquiries into the nature and origin of backwardness in reading. She suggests that complete illiterates who cannot master the mechanics of reading should be distinguished from slow readers with poor comprehension. Reading disability is varied in its causes and nature and should not be considered as a single disability of the same nature in all cases. There is no clear evidence of an inborn organic cause of the disability. And it is not always clear whether exceptional emotional characteristics cause the disability or result from it. "The one universal characteristic of non-readers suffering from specific reading disability is their complete failure to analyse word shapes and sounds systematically and associate them together correctly." In the worst cases the difficulties of reading may become too ingrained to be overcome. Where it is appropriate to use psychotherapy to remove emotional barriers to reading, this should be done. Meaningful learning based on children's interests should be associated with gradual advances in phonic analysis. If the phonic analysis is too stereotyped, or is unrelated to words that interest the child, or is introduced too soon, it may do more harm than good. It is difficult to assess teaching methods and remedial methods, but the reading standards achieved may vary widely from school to school, even in one social district.

Diagnosing the causes of backwardness in English composition, Schonell found that "as much backwardness was due to unsuitable teaching methods and to insufficient consideration of functional values as to paucity of experiences or to mental handicaps of the children." Here again the moral is the same. It is not sufficient to think of any topic and ask a class to write compositions on it. Have they any experience of the topic? Have they had the chance to read about it? Have they the reading ability to take advantage of such a chance? Are they interested in the topic? Do they see any point in writing about it? In many cases these questions would have to be answered in the negative. It may be regrettable to surrender the intention of setting a composition on some general topic, or to exercise the children in punctuation or paragraphing, but it would seem that these laudable aims have a better chance of success where the children have begun to see some point in them and to have something they want to write about.

Once a backward child has set out on the road of progress, the essential method of teaching him is to plan a carefully and slowly graded programme of work, and to praise his successes rather than condemn any failures. The scholastic part of the work should be limited severely in favour of practical work of all kinds. A bright retarded

child may make quite rapid progress, but the backward
child must be expected to hasten slowly. Otherwise he will
soon be experiencing again the pressures and the reproaches
which were his undoing in the first instance. If this
remedial policy seems too demanding of patience the
solution is to avoid the necessity for an exceptional output
of patience by exercising a reasonable degree of patience
in the first education of backward children. Hill (1939)
found that "13 per cent. of the seniors and 15 per cent. of
the juniors are children who, at the time of promotion
from department to department, are still needing the
instruction more commonly afforded in the department
they are leaving."

In an educational system where children advance
according to their chronological age, there is always a
proportion of children at each level who are not ready to
do the work of that level. It still has to be recognized that
there is a standing need for some secondary-school teachers
who will continue to teach primary-school reading and
arithmetic to the minority who need it, and junior-school
teachers who will similarly accept responsibility for work
that *cannot* be completed in the infant classes. The need
can be met only by co-operative effort. If the teacher is to
relax the normal scholastic pressures on the backward child
he must be supported by the headmaster, by the education
authority, and by parents. If the teacher is to have confidence in the general efficacy of the methods described in
this chapter there must be a child-guidance service and
special teachers for the worst cases which defy the class
teacher's best endeavours. All these requirements are
hindered by shortages of staff or material. This does not
justify losing sight of the goal which the evidence indicates
to be the right one.

The Freudians' emphasis on the power of hidden emotions,
Bartlett's conception of the transforming nature of the

human mind, the learning theorists' emphasis on reward and on new structurings, the testers' intellectual and educational assessments all have a bearing on this problem of backwardness. Later discussion of certain aspects of the psychology of human personality and development will make still clearer the relationship between general psychological topics and specific educational problems.

Chapter Seven

Discipline, Delinquency, and Deprivation

W HERE discipline is a problem young teachers are most concerned to find a solution, for failure to do so prevents progress in ordinary work. Similarly, where delinquency is a problem in a society, law-abiding citizens cast around for a whipping-boy or, if they are more rational, for causes and cures. There is no simple psychological formula for dealing with either of these practical problems, but psychological studies have thrown light on some areas that were formerly dark. Nowhere is it clearer that serious practical problems have to be solved by relating them to wider considerations than may seem relevant at first sight.

A young teacher may very naturally be so preoccupied with his own preparation and performance that he is disturbed by the capacity of a class of lively children to see the lesson in a different light from that intended and studiously planned. This has been epitomized in the saying that, to teach John Latin, you must know John as well as Latin. Controversy has continued on the question of how far the Latin is to be tailored to suit John, and how far John has to trim himself to fit the Latin. The traditional view ensured that John accommodated himself to what was prescribed or was soundly whipped (or caned or strapped or paddled, according to national taste). In the opposite view, held and practised by some modern educators, traditional curricula and methods should be radically changed, or even abolished, rather than maintained by corporal punishment. Many intermediate viewpoints are taken. The trend of practice has been away from corporal punishment, but those farthest away from immediate classroom problems have been readier than class teachers to reject corporal punishment in all situations. In countries or areas where corporal punishment has been banned there are often other strong sanctions to conform. These may be, for example, reports to parents on unsatisfactory work or conduct, or social and educational propaganda so strong that defiance of it leads to ostracism. Where these sanctions too are weak, then the educational standards achieved are liable to be lower than in a system which effectively sanctions educational effort and progress.

Disciplinary problems cannot be solved by simple rules or devices but only by understanding. Many have learned to see this educational problem as a choice between corporal punishment and 'free discipline.' But 'free discipline' can be as cramping and devastating as severe corporal punishment if it means letting children do what they want, either in the sense of what they happen to be doing in fact before an adult intervenes, or what they *say* they want when the adult asks them. Each of these criteria may be relevant, but there is the further criterion of what they would enjoy and profit from in response to the teacher's skilful stimulation and guidance. This is the critical educational criterion. Knowledge about the right stages and methods of leading different classes of children on to fresh pastures can be gathered and imparted, but the skill of applying the knowledge can be acquired only in practice. Psychological studies of child development and of learning provide the teacher with background and clues, but these cannot be expected to give immediate successes. Time and experience must go with them. This implies that one of the fundamental methods of discipline is patience in the teacher.

Psychological learning theories often stress reward as an essential ingredient in the learning process. Human beings, fortunately, have remarkable capacities for effort without immediate or constant reward, but learning must ultimately and in general be a rewarding situation if a child, or anyone else, is to be interested in it. Indiscipline is like backwardness in sometimes being a sign that the learning situation is devoid of this essential rewarding quality. The learner may be pressed beyond his general or specific abilities and interests. Indiscipline is his rebellion against an unfair deal. The solution is to give a fair deal, as suggested in the discussion of backwardness. Success must be engineered and commended. Failures and rebellious behaviour may have to be temporarily overlooked; otherwise they may be strengthened by their power to gain attention. In behavioural terms, the undesired responses must be extinguished by not being rewarded or reinforced. It is not enough that they are unrewarded in the obvious sense. They must be allowed to acquire a neutral, uninteresting quality, while desired responses are given attention and reward.

This may require a period when the child is freed from all the scholastic pressures that are associated with his troublesome behaviour. This therapeutic method is interestingly described by Burn (1956) in his account of G. A. Lyward's work at Finchden Manor. Children's lives may have been so 'usurped' by inappropriate people and purposes that they need complete respite from lessons as such. At Finchden these seriously disturbed boys "found security, emotional security from exterior pressures; from the mother who had badgered them with her griefs and the father with his ambition: security from ideals and immediate goals. No one judged them."

The main groups of factors influencing what happens in a classroom could be listed as follows :

(1) The teacher's knowledge of children and the subjects of study, and skill in handling both.

(2) The child's individual abilities and interests, general and specific.

(3) The atmosphere prevailing in the school, encouraging or discouraging various habits and attitudes (the Head's special responsibility).

(4) The atmosphere, psychological and physical, prevailing in the child's home, reinforcing or conflicting with the school's standards.

(5) The general social atmosphere, with its differing assumptions about what really matters and its pressures to conform with prevailing assumptions.

These varied sources of inconsistency in values and discipline have only to be listed to make it evident that poor discipline has many potential sources, and that some teachers inevitably have to crack harder nuts than others. While it is fair to recognize that there are sources of indiscipline which are in the nature of social rather than specifically educational problems, the teacher in the classroom still has a special rôle to fill because of his official responsibility and because of his own abilities and education. Morris (1955) has suggested that "*in loco parentis* is not just a legal idea" as far as teachers are concerned. Instead, the teacher may be for the child a new embodiment of the parent. If the natural parents are authoritarian or easy-going or variable in their discipline the child will half expect the teacher to be the same and half hope that he will be different. It depends on the teacher's psychological insight to determine what will help each child most. Sudden changes are probably best avoided, but the child who has suffered from lax discipline has to learn slowly the value of something more stringent; and equally, the child of authoritarian parents has to learn to be free. This is a rough guide. The child may have a more complicated problem to solve if his mother and father themselves diverge seriously in habits of discipline. Happy the child whose mother, father, and teacher concur in a moderate and enlightened discipline!

The above comments envisage an inhumanly wise and detached teacher. In practice the teacher too is deeply influenced by the kinds of discipline he experienced at home and school. It is like the old situation where the master kicks the servant and the servant kicks the dog. We tend to pass on to the world the treatment that it has meted out to us. The hope is that the power of reflection which men have may enable them to discharge some of their rancours or grievances in discussion before they act upon them. If a teacher was brought up in an authoritarian or indulgent or variable atmosphere he may have difficulty in achieving that sense of inward security which would enable him to dispense with authoritarianism, or self-indulgence, or wavering between uncertain standards. One of the virtues of a good college is to help each student to find a new security, and consequently a new perspective, if he needs it. The basic problems are common to all, but those who experience them in milder forms are abler to help others. While the experience of consistent affection and friendliness is the most effective aid to achieving security, intellectual understanding too can make some contribution.

Indiscipline is not now so often thought of as wilful rebellion but rather as a symptom of some maladjustment: that is, of some failure to live happily and constructively with the demands and the limitations of the environment and of one's own nature. It is a principle of common sense, although often neglected, that it is better to treat causes than symptoms. This is the main tenor of psychological thought on the topic of discipline. It should not obscure the fact that much indiscipline is both of a minor nature and not associated with anything worthy of being called maladjustment. A sensible teacher would not search for deep causes when some accident of circumstances, some efflorescence of high spirits, or some momentary naughtiness was sufficient explanation.

There are various local or special rules about corporal punishment. Perhaps one set of rules may be mentioned to illustrate a practical policy for a special purpose. The Home Office Regulations for the Administration of Children's Homes (1951) decree that no child under 10 shall be corporally punished except by smacking his hands with the bare hand of the person administering the punishment; the person in charge of the home only may cane a boy aged between 10 and 15; no girl over 10, nor boy over school-leaving age, may receive corporal punishment; no caning may be administered in the presence of another child; and only the medical officer has the power to sanction any corporal punishment at all for a child known to have any physical or mental disability. These regulations are for a specific set of circumstances and are quoted only to illustrate the kind of practice that may be sanctioned. If the diversity of aims and conditions of infant schools, primary schools, modern, technical, and grammar schools is considered the possibility of justifying very varied regulations is obvious. Each teacher has to consider for himself how far corporal punishment may be inimical to the instilling of humane principles, even where such punishment may seem most justified, and where the pupil may be quite free from maladjustment and apparently ready to accept his fate.

The child who runs foul of the teacher may be counted indisciplined. The child who runs foul of the law becomes a delinquent. Burt (1925) published the first large-scale English study of young delinquents. His data consisted of 200 consecutive cases of juvenile delinquency studied individually by himself, and as a control group he had 400 non-delinquent children of the same age, social class, and school as the delinquents. As in his study of general backwardness, this device ensured that he could see which factors were distinctively associated with delinquency. Again the fact of multiple causation was evident. The delinquent group, on the average, appeared to suffer from two and a half adverse congenital factors, and from seven adverse factors that were not congenital. This may be contrasted with the average of only one adverse congenital factor and only two and a half adverse non-congenital factors in the non-delinquent control group. Among the major factors, those that were environmental played a dominant rôle. The single factor most highly correlated with delinquency was defective discipline, but this was closely associated with many others. The group of causes that seemed paramount consisted of intellectual dullness (but not to the extent of mental deficiency), temperamental instability (but short of being pathological), defective family life, and harmful friendships formed outside the home. Together these accounted for 50 per cent. of the delinquencies and crimes.

Of Burt's delinquents 137 were followed up for twelve months or more. In about half of these cases suggested treatment was carried out, and in the other half it was not. Of those treated, 62 per cent. seemed cured, compared with 12 per cent. of the others. Of those treated, 36 per cent. made satisfactory but incomplete progress, compared with 23 per cent. of the others. Only 2 per cent. had wholly unsatisfactory reports, compared with 65 per cent. of those who did not have treatment. Burt made six general recommendations for dealing with juvenile delinquency:

(1) Early ascertainment is important, for moral character and temperamental eccentricity are founded in the pre-school years.

(2) The control of delinquency should be treated as one aspect of child welfare, for its problems overlap those of 'normal' development.

(3) Delinquency must be treated, not punished, and the treatment has to be individual.

(4) Remedies should be sought for the causes and not merely for the symptoms. This implies the availability of any necessary institutions for special purposes, and an adequate system of after-care for young people leaving such institutions.

(5) Research must be continued into cases and treatment.

(6) Delinquency should be prevented by the necessary programmes of social amelioration.

These recommendations still hold good, although they have all been put into practice to some extent since 1925.

Many American studies of delinquency have been published since Healy's *The Individual Delinquent* (1915). The Gluecks (1950) compared 500 persistent male delinquents with a control group of the same size. They summarize their findings thus:

The delinquents as a group are distinguishable from the non-delinquents: (1) *physically*, in being essentially meso-morphic in constitution (solid, close-knit, muscular); (2) *temperamentally*, in being restlessly energetic, impulsive, extroverted, aggressive, destructive (often sadistic)—traits which may be related more or less to the erratic growth pattern and its physiologic correlates or consequences; (3) *in attitude*, by being hostile, defiant, resentful, suspicious, stubborn, socially assertive, adventurous, unconventional, non-submissive to authority; (4) *psychologically*, in tending to direct and concrete, rather than symbolic, intellectual expression, and in being less methodical in their approach to problems; (5) *socio-culturally*, in having been reared to a far greater extent than the control group in homes of little understanding, affection, stability, or moral fibre, by parents usually unfit to be effective guides and protectors or, according to psychoanalytic theory, desirable sources for emulation and the construction of a consistent, well-balanced, and socially normal super-ego during the early stages of character development.[1]

Pearce (1952) concludes that two of the commonest features of the persistent delinquent are (a) that he has experienced prolonged separation from his mother before the age of 5, and (b) that he is "unwanted by parents who are themselves unstable and unhappy people and whose attitudes towards him are, on balance, hostile, critical, and punishing." Stott (1952) claims that "mere removal from the anxiety-creating situation is sufficient to restore the majority of approved school lads to common sense and stability." Stott (1956) describes twelve patterns of breakdown in family relationships which may give rise to different forms of maladjustment in the young. Juvenile delinquency may be caused by a concatenation of five circumstances :

(1) Social conditions giving rise to stresses and strains.
(2) An element of personality weakness in the parents.
(3) The experience of being deprived of consistent maternal affection, especially in infancy.
(4) The existence of a lax or apathetic social neighbourhood in which delinquency is condoned.
(5) The onset of some crisis which may be the last straw needed to break the camel's back.

Stott is critical of what he believes to be the traditional intellectual approach to diagnosing and treating delinquency and pleads for a "common-sense" recognition of the emotional basis of maladjustment and delinquency. The more the symptoms of maladjustment betray an intolerable family situation, the greater the need for the child's urgent withdrawal from it.

[1] From *Unraveling Juvenile Delinquency*, by permission of S. and E. Glueck, the Commonwealth Fund, and Harvard University Press.

Juvenile delinquency is very much commoner among boys than girls. The incidence rises to a peak about the age of 13, and the commonest offence is larceny. The second commonest is 'breaking and entering.' In England and Wales in 1958 the magistrates' courts dealt with over 28,000 indictable offences by children under 14, with over 22,000 by young persons between 14 and 16 inclusive, and over 16,000 by persons between 17 and 20 inclusive. The three main methods of disposing of those under 17 were probation (35 per cent.), conditional discharge (30 per cent.), and fining (15 per cent.). Those sent to approved schools constituted 5 per cent. of the group. Over 38,000 non-indictable offences by persons under the age of 17 were dealt with by fining (71 per cent.) or by discharge or probation. The incidence of delinquency varies from time to time in a way that is only broadly understood.

Various legal assumptions are made about children, although these may not be psychologically valid in every case. No child under 8 can be charged with a legal offence, and up to 14 the assumption continues in general that a child cannot have *mens rea*, a guilty mind. Up to the age of 16, all children and young persons must be dealt with by a juvenile court. Separate courts for juveniles were first legally sanctioned by the Children Act of 1908. Brief mention of some of the graver methods of disposing of cases of delinquency will show how the law attempts to cater for different kinds; the psychological principle applied (somewhat imperfectly) is that of segregating unlike cases which might be harmful to one another.

(1) Remand homes for local authority areas were made obligatory by the Children and Young Persons Act of 1933. They are for boys and girls up to the age of 17, and may be used as places of detention up to a maximum of one month, or as places of accommodation pending an

appearance in court or other consideration or disposal of a case.

(2) Attendance centres are for boys aged 12 but under 17, who may, for example, have to attend for two hours on each of six Saturdays, at fortnightly intervals. Usually, vigorous physical activity and craft work are used as part of the means of educating the boys in the constructive use of leisure.

(3) Detention centres, authorized by the Criminal Justice Act, 1948, are for offenders aged 14 but under 21. The maximum detention is six months. According to a Home Office report (1955), "the keynote of the régime is brisk activity under strict discipline and supervision."

(4) Approved schools are for those of 10 but under 17 years of age. Those under 15 may be committed for a maximum of three years or till 15 years 4 months, whichever is longer. Those over 15 may be committed for a maximum of three years or till 19, whichever is shorter.

(5) Borstals are for youths of 14 but under 21. The maximum period of committal is for three years. A juvenile court must send a case to Quarter Sessions (in England) before a Borstal committal can be made.

Borstals are of deliberately varied character, depending on what seems to be the best sifting out of those in need of their services. In both approved schools and Borstals there is considerable emphasis on crafts, physical exercise, sport, and vocational preparation. Mannheim and Wilkins (1955) have shown that 'open' Borstals, in which restriction is less severely imposed, have a higher success rate than 'closed' Borstals. This seems to be as true for those lads who have shown a poor chance of success as for those who have promised well at an early stage. The authors recommend that there should be regular statistical studies to show what factors known at earlier stages are correlated with success and failure at later stages. These correlations would not determine what was best for individual cases but, if kept up to date, would be valuable adjuncts to this purpose.

Bowlby (1951), reviewing studies of deprivation of affection in children, has shown how children brought up in institutions in infancy later score lower on tests of intelligence, education, social maturity, and capacity for personal relationships than children in foster-homes. There seems to be a greater tendency for children who have spent the first three years of life in an institution to be, at a later age, unpopular with other children, to be fearful and to crave affection, and to be restless and unable to concentrate. Bowlby lists, among the factors associated with deprivation, illegitimacy, unemployment, chronic illness, instability of parents, the absence in hospital of child or parents, the imprisonment of parents, separation, divorce, and the regular absence of the mother or father from home because of employment. Since Bowlby's publication the theme of deprivation has recurred in many others.

The Children Act, 1948, embodied some of the widespread feeling that more should be done to safeguard the welfare and happiness of children who have been deprived of normal parental care. Section I of this Act lays upon local authorities the duty of assuming the care of children "where it appears to a local authority with respect to a child in their area appearing to them to be under the age of 17 that he has neither parents nor guardian or has been and remains abandoned by his parents or guardian or is lost; or that his parents or guardian are, for the time being or permanently, prevented by reasons of mental or bodily disease or infirmity or other incapacity or any other circumstances from providing for his proper accommodation, maintenance, or upbringing." Section V of the Act makes it obligatory upon local authorities to undertake the care of a delinquent or imminently delinquent child in virtue of a 'fit person' order by a court. How can the local authority care for these classes of children?

The first endeavour is to facilitate the speedy return of the child to his own home if possible, for children may have a paradoxical devotion even to a bad or cruel home. The social worker's dilemma of deciding between the obvious evils of certain homes and the vital psychological function of the home in a child's development exemplifies the importance of a deep understanding of the psychology of the family. A second method is to place the child in a foster-home and pay the foster-parents for their services. The current view favours this semi-professional basis for fostering as being economically realistic and not, in practice, inconsistent with children's welfare. The difficulty about this method is to find sufficient foster-parents who will give the children loving attention while they need it without growing to depend on the children for their own emotional satisfaction. A third method, adoption, was legalized in England in 1926, and in Scotland in 1930. The number of adoptions in 1952 was 14,560 in England, and 1515 in Scotland. There are more prospective adopters than there are children available to be adopted. Many children who come into public care will sooner or later return to their own homes. Not every prospective adopter will be judged suitable to go through with the process. A fourth method of caring for children is in children's homes. In large homes the best will in the world is not enough to give a child the sense of individual love. The tendency is, therefore, to establish family group homes in which a house-mother will look after seven children, or a larger number where a compromise has to be accepted.

Where a child stands a chance of prospering in his own home, various welfare devices may help to rehabilitate the home. Measures that have been recommended include a home-help service for 'submerged' households, a greater emphasis on principles of psychological health in the education of health visitors, and some correlation of social welfare agencies so that a single family does not deal with a dozen different welfare agencies. Family Service Units in certain centres have sent out individual workers who enter actively into the rehabilitation of the most unfortunate and feckless families, not only giving advice but doing housework and restoring some sense of worthwhileness to the home.

The problems discussed in this chapter require to be considered with reference to their social and legal, as well as to their psychological, aspects. These social and legal aspects help one to understand how psychological ideas manifest themselves in public practice. Psychological inquiries of the statistical kind help to reveal the underlying causes of the problems, while studies in individual psychology, sometimes in accordance with psychoanalytic principles, illumine ordinary experience, even when they have not observed the strictest canons of scientific method.

Six practical implications for the young teacher may be worth mentioning.

(1) Where discipline is a problem the solution must be expected to take time.

(2) A teacher who finds his discipline much poorer than that of a colleague in similar circumstances may require to review his own attitudes, aims, and techniques.

(3) A good command of the material being taught is an important ingredient of good discipline.

(4) If indiscipline cannot be traced to mistaken teaching methods or aims within the classroom the causes may be found in the family or general social background of the child. Even where the teacher can do little to change these underlying influences, an understanding of them may lead to more mutual sympathy between teacher and taught.

(5) Success depends upon a proper balance between

making allowances for children's limitations and handicaps and at the same time giving them a firm lead into successful learning and good behaviour.

(6) Children whose behaviour requires them to be dealt with in any of the special ways mentioned in this chapter are typically the victims of circumstances. Scientific studies have suggested that security and affection in the family are more important circumstances than material wealth alone.

Chapter Eight

Æsthetic and Technical Education

STHETIC and technical education might at first sight seem to have little connection either with one another or with educational psychology. This is not entirely surprising when one considers the extent to which they are kept segregated both in practice and in discussion. The word 'æsthetic' is popularly associated with the fine arts, such as painting or sculpture, although it can be intelligently applied in a much wider variety of circumstances. The word 'technical' is popularly associated with practical efficiency and precision, especially in the setting of machines and workshops, although a much wider application is appropriate. The traditional tendency has been to define the æsthetic and the technical by reference to narrow and mutually exclusive ranges of human endeavour. The view suggested here is that almost every human activity has both an æsthetic and a technical side to it, a side that has to do with the feeling of a job being well or badly performed, and a side that has to do with the techniques or devices that enable the job to be done. A fine painting that conveys a pleasurable feeling to the inexpert viewer may also convey a sense of masterly techniques to the connoisseur. An engine that satisfies its user because it does efficiently what it is supposed to may give the person who made it or who understands it a sense of beauty in the aptness of its construction. The fact that the æsthetic and technical aspects can be and often are kept separate is not denied. What matters for educational and psychological development is that they need not be.

With this idea that the æsthetic and technical are complementary aspects of life, it is more readily seen that they can be considered with reference to the three 'R's' and, indeed, to any subject that is taught—and not only to those that have been traditionally labelled Art or Technical Subjects. What has been said about the practical problems of backwardness, discipline, and delinquency now fits into a broad psychological principle—namely, that a balance must always be maintained between the æsthetic and technical aspects of any learning. The technicalities of phonic analysis will bore and confuse a child who has not a feeling of pleasurable accomplishment in, and of self-committal to, the business of reading. Similarly, irregular French verbs, difficult Latin constructions, tricky geometrical problems, ambitious English compositions, will all be approached with more verve and efficiency if this balance is maintained. The persisting aims and methods of much of the educational system militate strongly against this principle. Even where lip-service is paid to the principle, the practical pressures of parents and examinations and school prestige cause teachers to advance the presentation of technicalities beyond the learners' genuine feeling for the subject. The learners do make a forced progress, although many turn their backs at last on the intellectual meal which has sickened them.

The fact that the technical has tended to outstrip the æsthetic in the past should not cause anyone to slide into the opposite error of under-emphasizing the technical. This has happened where teachers have come to believe that modern educational method consists in letting children do what they want. Rousseau, the very father of modern educational psychology, made no mistake here. Children were to feel that they were doing what they wanted, but the educator was to contrive that their activities would be in accordance with what he judged good for them. In school, children must often be set to master technical skills before they have any enthusiasm for acquiring them. The activity may have to be tried and savoured before æsthetic satisfaction is possible at all. Children have to be subtly stimulated without being penalized if they fail to rise to the first bait. Sometimes it helps to point out the utility or pleasure of a certain activity, if these are genuine and not mere fabrications. Sometimes the chance of voluntarily choosing the activity must be offered several times. Sometimes the activity may have to be accepted arbitrarily, but soon the teacher will give a surprising demonstration of what pleasure it can give. The teacher's own desire to have a child share his skill and knowledge will win many to hard endeavour if the teacher's desire is sincere rather than simulated. The teacher will develop professional techniques of engaging children's interest and effort in so far as he searches for the æsthetic satisfaction of his own work. This professional satisfaction is not a question of feeling some out-of-the-blue 'vocation' to teach, but of sensing how children can be beguiled into developing their best selves.

While children have possibilities of æsthetic development in all their work, it is not without reason that certain parts of the curriculum have been expected traditionally to make a special contribution. The pictorial and plastic creations of young children are a matter of common knowledge and delight. Young children revel in papers and crayons and paints and "Plasticine" and sand and water, and in bits and pieces of all kinds. Their creations often have a freshness and vivacity and untutored flair for design that are less commonly attained in adolescence. Their well-known habit of representing what they know to be there even when some of the items cannot be seen in 'reality' suggests how, at an early stage in development, the intellect is as active as the senses in making a picture of the world. Children also project their personal concerns, absorptions, joys, and anxieties, although these cannot be interpreted mechanically, but only in the light of other information. Where an adult might express some personal problem by discussing it repeatedly with friends and neighbours (this accounting for a considerable proportion of our adult conversation), a child does so in a "Plasticine" model or in a drawing.

The vitality of children's creations and their psychological significance might lead one to expect that teachers must long have harnessed them in the cause of educational development. They have; but often with a heavy harness of technical instruction and adult objectives that have pulled children back to a slow drag. Too early copying of models or studying the rules of perspective have impeded or prevented the personal vision which gives distinction to artistic endeavour. In technical education at the secondary-school level, traditional exercises have been arbitrarily set, even when their purposes could equally be achieved by other creations, in which the children could choose and themselves use the products. Mechanical practice is necessary but it need not be mechanically obtained. The multiplication tables can be memorized by solving a multitude of little problems in which they are needed, as well as by chanting them aloud. The making of a particular woodwork joint can be embodied in producing an object that does or does not matter to a boy. Recent decades have witnessed a steady move towards freeing children from a premature methodology, but still over-emphasis of the grammar of subjects tends to detract from their educative effect. A grammatical approach can be learned by heart. To discipline children's work by individual challenge is much harder work, especially in large classes. Not enough has yet been done to help teachers with the detailed practical problems of applying good methods in difficult circumstances. Some teachers give up the methods, but some adapt them with ingenuity and courage.

At one level children's æsthetic development consists in exploring the world physically—touching, manipulating, constructing, and destroying. Even some of their psychological explorations flow through physical activities in playing at schools, houses, jobs, and so on. But much of their development depends upon the wider explorations made possible by literature. Nursery stories feed the infant's mind. Romantic tales, whether fictitious or historical, extend the child's conception of the physical world and of the people in it. They provide models with which the child may identify himself, and thus contribute to his moral education. Encouragement in oral and written composition offer him a more advanced (if also more difficult) means of controlling his intellectual and emotional world. Listening to, or making, poetry and music can heighten a developing sensitivity to things which are both enjoyable and illuminating.

All these means of education are liable to fail if the teacher's manner or the demands of examinations interfere with the immediacy of the æsthetic experience. In secondary schools, because of the heavier technical demands made upon the children, there is a greater risk that the imaginative subjects, or the imaginative aspects of more technical studies, may be ousted. Wall (1955) regrets the way in which creative activities "are regarded as frills and are often the first victims of overcrowding in the timetable or shortage of staff or of money." The adolescent, like the younger child, and like the adult, should be enabled to discover what is worth while *for him* in music, literature, and art, rather than coached into pseudo-appreciations of works which do not touch his heart. And he should be encouraged in acquiring practical skills, which are a solace to healthy men and women, just as they are a recognized means of therapy for those who have been mentally distressed.

Several features seem to be characteristic of creative activity. The creator is given the opportunity of wide studies in his field. He has time to digest his studies and to make them part of himself. He feels challenged by a problem, an idea, or a vision. He has time to mull it over. Then, fluently or haltingly, he expresses it in his own medium. The variety of detail is great, but, typically, it takes time to create something personal that expresses and enriches the character of the creator. The modern idea of art education is to give children some of the above conditions of work so that they have the best chance of achieving something valuable. An interest in the appearance and design of everything around them will be cultivated. A great variety of materials and techniques will be shown, thus increasing the chance that one or more of these may captivate. There is an opportunity of achieving something whose concreteness is more readily appreciated by a young or less academic person, and which imposes its own discipline rather than the discipline of any particular person. The systematic grammar of any medium will be mainly for advanced students.

Peter Slade (1954) has practised and expounded a psychologically based view of the place of child drama in education. The general view is grounded firstly in observation and practice, but the theory is psychological. A central idea is that there must be a balance between what he calls In-flow and Out-flow. In-flow is "the taking in of ideas and experiences," and Out-flow is "the pouring out of creative forms of expression, a tendency which can be regulated and encouraged, and which by frequent opportunity becomes a habit promoting confidence." A simple and common example of these phenomena is the young child who, having had some momentous personal experience at home or in the playground, may be incapable of taking in the teacher's instruction until he has expressed to the latter the wonderful thing that fills his mind. Another striking, if grim, example of necessary Out-flow was shown in the French film *Les Jeux Interdits* (*Secret Game*), where a little girl whose parents had been killed during the War expressed her inner tension in funeral games. Slade's view is that children should be encouraged to participate in improvised drama which provides a legitimate and creative outlet for inner emotions. This dramatic education may begin in a music-and-movement way. Children are invited to move about an open space to varied sounds and rhythms, to be trees or wild bears or anything that seems suitable to the teacher. Later the children will make their own playlets, which may be quite short and quite different from the tidy versions which some adults impose upon children. An essential part of the method is that the teacher should not dominate the children with his own suggestions or ideas. He may throw out ideas to start the ball rolling, but they should be quite general and their transformation or rejection by the children should not be discouraged.

Slade's views are impressive because they give such clear and reasoned scope to free expression on the one hand and to a developing discipline on the other. The teacher helps the developing discipline by means of suggestions, but does not impose it by giving orders or showing displeasure at some unconventional pattern. The children are not allowed to persist in any behaviour which interferes gravely with the freedom of others. Such behaviour is likely to arise only where the method is introduced to older children accustomed to very different ways. A wide range of merits is claimed for child drama, including the provision of a legitimate outlet for emotions that might diminish a child's scholastic efficiency or turn it to delinquency, and the development of speech, memory, understanding, imagination, sincerity, confidence, and spontaneity. The study of Slade's book, with its wealth of concrete illustrations, suggests that these claims are not too optimistic, provided that child drama is thought of as one contribution among others to an education based on the study of children's natures.

There has been widespread recognition of the need to make all education at once liberal and technical, but both the kind of education traditionally considered liberal and the kind considered technical have tended to go on being technical. It may seem most difficult of all to make traditional technical education anything more than a training in practical skills directed to specific utilitarian purposes. Dobinson (1951) suggests that secondary schools should accept the frankly vocational interests and aspirations of many pupils as the central educational consideration. A liberal influence would be exerted—firstly, by developing outward, but not too far away, from a core of vocational preparation; and secondly, by making only a few teachers responsible for the entire education of the boys and girls. The first measure would mean that, for example, the whole range of world literature would be drawn upon rather than a few traditional English authors, and that books would be more closely related to what really interests adolescents. The limitation of the number of teachers handling a class would facilitate a more consistent and inter-related presentation of worth-while knowledge and attitudes.

Venables (1955), discussing the needs and problems of technical students, emphasizes the great diversity of talents and motives among the students. He notes the common hostility among them towards everything reminiscent of a school atmosphere. Their purposes are primarily vocational or recreative. They need educational, vocational, and personal guidance of a non-didactic kind. They need to be considered as individuals. Brown (1954) argues that many attitudes and forms of behaviour that were once thought to be part of unchanging 'human nature' are now known to vary with environmental circumstances. In industry the material environment and social welfare services have been vastly improved, but this has not always produced the greatest efficiency and harmony, for a genuine and persistent human concern and consideration for individuals may still be absent. Such concern and consideration may depend on decentralizing industrial control so that, at each level, workers and managers can meet one another face to face, and be responsible for resolving their own problems. This corresponds to giving more responsibility to individual teachers and Heads in a school system. Oakley (1945) reinforces this general argument in his discussion of training young workers. These must be placed in jobs for which they are most suited, encouraged to learn about, and identify themselves with, the aims of their industry, and trained in the detailed technical methods which have been shown on analysis to be most efficient. These writers, versed in the practical problems of technical education and of vocational requirements, show a considerable degree of concurrence in the main argument of this chapter—that even technical education in the narrow sense depends for its efficiency, let alone for its potentially educative influence, on taking stock of the psychology of the learners. Economical work techniques alone or psychological insight alone are not enough. Both must be brought together, so that a developing feel for the work (the æsthetic side) whets the appetite for efficient methods (the technical side).

In technical education, as in other kinds, efficient guidance of people into the courses that best match their abilities and aptitudes is a vital part of educational method.

Popular discussion might suggest that selecting learners and teaching them were two unconnected processes, whereas good selection should rather be counted an essential part of good teaching method. Much experimentation has been done on recognizing various technical aptitudes. Paper and pencil tests have been used in which mechanical and geometrical problems have to be solved. Assembly tests have been used to find whether a candidate can assemble an electric bell or perform some similar mechanical operation. Interest tests have been used to test whether a candidate has the pattern of interests that is known to be characteristic of a machine-operator, or a salesman, or any other general kind of worker. The National Institute of Industrial Psychology sometimes uses a seven-point survey of :

(1) physical make-up;
(2) attainments;
(3) general intelligence;
(4) special aptitudes;
(5) interests;
(6) disposition;
(7) circumstances.

A rough way of considering temperamental factors is to judge whether a candidate would be happiest working directly with people (like a teacher), indirectly with people (like some administrators), directly with things (like a mason), or indirectly with things (like a designer). The ranges of general intelligence found in separate jobs overlap extensively, but the general level of intelligence required for particular jobs is known.

One systematic technique of vocational guidance depends on analysing the qualities required for every job available, and then devising tests of the separate qualities. This is a useful conception, but lack of a wide variety of reliable and valid tests and the need to make relatively quick decisions commonly necessitate a more rule-of-thumb procedure. Researches have shown that deliberately planned vocational guidance tends to pay. Those who follow the recommendations of vocational counsellors tend to hold their jobs longer, feel happier in them, and earn more money. Dobinson advocates more continuous and thorough vocational guidance of secondary-school children after the French fashion, so that educational and vocational decisions are not based on irrelevant influences.

Given that a person has accepted good vocational advice, so that the job matches his abilities and circumstances, it pays to follow the good selection with good training. According to Ghiselli and Brown (1955),

> a review of the results of training programmes in industry revealed the following : increased worker satisfaction, higher levels of morale, increased interest in the work, closer co-operation between management and the workers, reduction in sick-time, reduction in absenteeism, improved safety records, increased level of output, reduced variation in output, and decreased labour turnover.

This is not only a testimony to the benefit of training but also an indication of the specific criteria by which improvements may be measured.

Much experimental work has been done on the learning of skills such as typing or performing various industrial operations. From it the following principles have been established :

(1) Even after trainees have been selected individual differences are found in their initial performances, in their rates of learning, and in their final performances. This should not surprise a teacher, but it is a reminder of the persistent importance of individual training. It is particularly relevant to working out realistic goals for different persons and encouraging them to accept these.

(2) It is more economic of time and effort to help trainees with demonstrations, explanations, and guidance rather than let them muddle about unguided. As a corollary, they ought to be kept informed of their own results, for otherwise they will be slower to learn.

(3) There is general agreement that learning is better if practice periods are reasonably spaced out. The actual spacing depends on circumstances, but, as an example, a half-hour on each of six consecutive days would often be better than one and a half hour's practice on Monday followed by another hour and a half on Saturday. 'Teach Yourself' books emphasize the superiority of doing a little regularly rather than attempting a lot at lengthy intervals.

(4) It seems, too, that where there is a close functional relationship between the different parts of a skill it is better to learn the tasks as a whole rather than in parts. This assumes that the task is not too big to be gone through at once. It would be better, with a short poem or piece of music, to go through the whole six times, rather than learn several subdivisions independently.

In the classroom the above principles would mean (a) that the teacher would regularly cater for individual differences rather than regard them as an irritating irregularity; (b) that he would not leave children fumbling too long without help and explanation, nor too long without being told their results; (c) that he would favour the policy of a little often rather than a lot occasionally; and (d) that, where the size of a task allowed, he would at least give some sense of the whole before proceeding to detailed study of the parts.

If a learner's progress in acquiring a skill is plotted on a graph the improvement is striking at the beginning, but often the learning curve levels off to what is called a learning plateau. This is a period of no manifest progress, when, perhaps, the first achievements are being consolidated. It may take some time, or possibly some further advice and guidance, before the curve of improvement again rises. Teacher and learner are helped by the knowledge that the learning plateau is usual, and that continuous manifest progress is not to be expected. It is so natural to forget the trials and tribulations of beginning to acquire a new skill. The teacher must reflect on his more *recently* acquired skills (dancing, swimming, driving, or teaching itself, perhaps) in order to have a sympathetic feel for all beginners.

There is the varying degree of confidence in the outcome of the first efforts. There is a seeking for success, for a word of encouragement. There is the tense, earnest attention of the learner driver and the alarmingly imperfect co-ordination that echoes in the grinding of gears. There is the difficulty in doing so many things at once—clutch and gear and brake and mirror and signal, etc. And yet when the parts of the skill come together the driver relaxes, converses, and wonders what all the difficulty was. The paradox of acquiring skills is that the beginner's earnest attentiveness produces a crude performance, while the master's finished performance seems unthinking.

Changes in æsthetic and technical education have often sprung from practical experience or economic considerations. Practical psychological help and general psychological theorizing have sometimes come along in the rear. Now the casual and empirical are thoroughly intermingled with the systematic and scientific. Psychologists have contributed to the improvement of technical designs and processes by analysing these in relation to human users. They have improved methods of guiding the right people to the right jobs and courses. These results are perhaps most tangible and therefore most easily appreciated. Less tangible, but no less vital, are certain features of development and learning which have been shown to be of practical and theoretical importance. Let us review these with reference to the psychology of learning to read, for reading is one of the most fundamental skills. The process of acquiring this skill is itself both technical and æsthetic; and the skill when acquired contributes to technical and æsthetic development.

Firstly, human learning is greatly facilitated when there exists what has been called 'ego-involvement.' This means that the learner is not only outwardly absorbed in the activity, but in a sense absorbs the whole activity into himself as part of what he intimately values. Such absorption may be stimulated or engineered to a certain extent, but depends on self-committal and may be hindered by outside pressure. In learning to read, the prerequisites of the child's self-committal and progress include (a) familiarity with the spoken use of common words which may occur in the reading lessons; (b) the ability to express ideas, tell stories, follow the tales of others, answer questions, etc.; (c) the ability to identify and distinguish visual shapes; (d) the ability to accept the social situation of school life; and (e) the desire to learn to read. A teacher has to make sure of the preceding ground before advancing into the mechanics of reading. Tests of reading readiness are designed to assess children's development in such areas.

Secondly, the first steps into the techniques of a skill should be made with suitably simple material. There should be enough repeated practice to allow familiarity and confidence to grow. And there should be enough relation of the practice to the learner's interests to maintain the absorption which was carefully encouraged at the first stage. In learning to read, short familiar words are used in a variety of settings. The child's interest in the words may be based on their reference to common features of his world, or on their association with interesting stories. As he comes to recognize a small stock of such words, the child is encouraged in the feeling that reading does bring satisfaction and progress. Words that have occurred in the stories and word games of the pre-reading preparation are discovered again in the reading primer, thus building up the learner's confidence. All the time there is emphasis upon making reading meaningful rather than mechanical.

Thirdly, the further development of the skill should take account of any available systematic analysis of its nature. Time-and-motion study in industry has attempted to eliminate unnecessary movements and obstacles. Gilbreth and Carey's *Cheaper by the Dozen* is an amusing biography of one of the pioneers in this field. In reading, it is known that the eyes move along the print in a series of jerks, making stops or fixations at several points in the line. Reading can take place only during the fixations. Gray (1956) shows how a good reader may read a line of print with only three fixations, while a poor reader may take as many as twenty fixations to the same line. Similarly, a good reader's fixations tend to be shorter in duration, and he has less need to look back. His eyes jerk regularly from left to right, except when moving back to the beginning of the next line of print. In the encouragement of left-to-right movement the teacher profits from our understanding of the physical process of reading. Reading material that includes many unfamiliar words, or is difficult to understand, or is badly set out, will hinder the teacher's purpose. More intelligent or knowledgeable children will, of course, have an inevitable advantage. Children of less intelligence or poorer verbal background need most help.

The study of typical reading errors has suggested what difficulties must be anticipated. Words of similar visual pattern like 'bad' and 'bed' may be confused, and therefore are better introduced separately from one another. Pairs of letters like 'b' and 'd' or 'p' and 'q' are readily confused by some children. Words like 'was' and 'saw' are another source of confusion. This reminds us that it can be as big a problem for a child to make such visual distinctions as it is for the uninitiated adult to decipher a menu in French or to take the right turning at a complicated roundabout. The phonic difficulties of a language with words like 'through,' 'dough,' and 'rough' are well recognized and necessitate appropriate graded training.

Fourthly, whether one is learning to read, typewrite, swim, or operate a lathe, the training must develop towards independence. This aim is a further sanction for encouraging understanding and genuine interest throughout. A mechanical, uninterested performance is of much less value, for it cannot be counted on to vary intelligently according to the circumstances, nor to persist reliably when it may be needed. Intelligence and interest in the learner are greatest when the teacher himself is skilful and genuinely interested. There is no substitute for genuinely good teachers. As the learner acquires independent mastery of the skill, he can use it for his own enrichment without constant guidance. The person who has learned to read can go far beyond the first lessons in æsthetic and moral values. For him the open book is a world.

This chapter might be summed up in terms of 'expression,' 'discipline,' and 'development.' Briefly, young people express their feelings, ideas, problems, and imaginings in various ways which have the quality of play. As they grow older the expression tends to move from more concrete media to the medium of words. It is possible to influence such expressions so that they take creative and delightful forms which encourage technical advances, or, alternatively, so that they are suppressed. In the second case there is at least the possibility that the suppressed material will inhibit technical advances in school subjects, and may eventually burst out in delinquent forms. Advocacy of self-expression has given rise to a false assumption that discipline should be minimal or non-existent. Discipline is essential to educational progress, and in some actual situations has to be severer than may be necessary in others. This does not detract from the merit and occasional practicability of a more refined conception of discipline as a gradual acceptance of added restraints, imposed, not by a teacher's arbitrary authority, but by successive self-committals to tasks which give an over-all balance of success. This is analogous to the discipline which the stone imposes on the mason; but the teacher still plays an active, although non-dominating, part. In the secondary school, or earlier, children are normally committed to extensive skill-acquiring programmes of work. Much wastage of ability arises from taking the committal for granted, when a very little attention to cultivating a sense of significance would rescue studies from aridity. At the same time the teacher should make use of what is known about the technical aspects of acquiring skills.

The study of children's development reveals natural tendencies to enjoy intensely certain aspects of what they sense or imagine. It also reveals a natural enjoyment of handling things. These are the starting-point of all æsthetic and technical education. Work that has been done in diverse, and often difficult, situations suggests that these features of natural development can be cultivated and enriched by humane and skilful teaching, and that the humane discipline which is needed in the classroom is also needed in the technical college and the factory.

Chapter Nine

Personality

I N discussions of educational method it is often said that
what really matters is the personality of the teacher.
This belief has been reasserted in the preceding discussion of how psychology applies to various practical
problems. Teachers are required to assess children's
personalities for report cards or for promotion recommendations or in vocational references. Apart from these
formal requirements, a teacher's insight into his own
personality and into the personality of others is a great
potential source of success and happiness for all concerned.
It has become increasingly clear that intellectual, academic,
and utilitarian conceptions of the educational process have
to be supplemented by a larger recognition of the way in
which emotional, temperamental, and similar aspects of
human nature enter into all learning. Personality has
increased in importance at the level of aims as well as of
methods. The full development of personality and the
development of the best aspects of personality have been
prominent ideas in educational writings. Against this background the need stands out clearly to study such questions
as how personality can be defined, how far it is innate or
how far acquired, how it can be assessed, and how it can be
changed.

Sometimes 'personality' means the superficial impression
made on us by a person. In this sense personality varies
widely with the beholder. Those personalities that make
the greatest display of themselves may impress people

forcibly, although an unobtrusive personality may be more genuinely distinctive and forcible. Personality is sometimes conceived in moral terms. As the assessment will vary according to the different moral standards that may be applied, it is more useful to associate the word 'character' with this aspect of personality. Psychologists have tended to use the word 'personality' in a more comprehensive sense. A good and typical example is the definition by H. J. Eysenck (1953). "Personality is the more or less stable and enduring organization of a person's character, temperament, intellect, and physique, which determines his unique adjustment to the environment." This definition includes two important points. It indicates that personality has to do with persisting patterns in a person's behaviour, but recognizes that these may change to some extent. And it specifies four main areas of comparison, while recognizing that the possible admixtures of elements are sufficiently varied to render each individual in some fashion unique. *Character* is the striving; and potentially moral, aspect of personality; *temperament* the affective or emotional aspect; *intellect* the cognitive and ideational aspect; and *physique* the bodily aspect, including nervous and glandular as well as bony and muscular structure.

One of the oldest and most persistent approaches to personality is that of typology, the attempt to classify people into a limited number of types. This attempt has often been made in terms of physical types, perhaps because this gives an apparently substantial foundation to typology, or because it is easier to note physical differences (at least, superficially) than others more recondite. The best-known traditional classification of this kind implied that various physical 'humours' determined individual temperament. The four main kinds were the sanguine, melancholic, choleric, and phlegmatic, responsible respectively for moving a person towards cheerful optimism, sad pessimism, irascibility, and unemotional detachment.

Comparable modern typologies are associated with the names of Kretschmer, Jung, and Sheldon. Kretschmer was a pioneer in correlating bodily appearances with psychological characteristics. He used the terms *asthenic, athletic,* and *pyknic* to distinguish what Sheldon later called *ectomorphic, mesomorphic,* and *endomorphic* types. Jung did much to develop the ideas of *extraversion* and *introversion,* and to explore the psychological ramifications of this distinction between the outward-turning and inward-turning personalities. He argued that extraversion and introversion exist in each person. The obviously sociable person has a retiring aspect to his personality; the obviously retiring person conceals a yearning to turn outward and be sociable. The two types are further differentiated in terms of thinking, feeling, sensation, and intuition. For example, the extravert-thinking type tends to be dominated by the objective situation as he sees it. He will do wrong in order to achieve what he has formulated as right. His doubts are converted into fanaticism. The introvert-thinking type, on the other hand, seems indifferent to the object of his thought. His work is scrupulous but his expression is complicated. He tends to be misunderstood, and yet is better liked as he becomes better known. Sheldon and his followers assessed the physical and temperamental characteristics of a large number of young men. The physical characteristics are considered in three sections : *ectomorphy* is the relative degree of development of the body's nervous tissue; *mesomorphy* is the relative degree of development of the body's muscular tissue; and *endomorphy* is the relative degree of development of the body's fatty tissue. Each of these was rated on a seven-point scale. A person whose combined rating was 4–4–4 would represent average development of all three physical aspects. Sheldon claimed further that a predominantly ectomorphic body tends to be associated with an intellectual and inward-looking temperament; a predominantly mesomorphic body with a sports-loving, activity-seeking temperament; and a predominantly endomorphic body with an easy-going, pleasure-seeking temperament. These associations have popular analogues in the stereotypes of the thin, withdrawn intellectual; the well-built, muscular outdoor type; and the fat, cheerful person. Shakespeare's Julius Caesar made such distinctions in the lines :

> Let me have men about me that are fat;
> Sleek-headed men and such as sleep o' nights.
> Yond Cassius has a lean and hungry look;
> He thinks too much : such men are dangerous.

While there is some association between physical appearance and temperament, it is hardly big enough to be of much practical use. In one study of the Sheldon kind the highest correlation was under $+0.4$. Sheldon's own work has also been criticized on the grounds that the ratings of physique and temperament were not made independently, that the statistical reliability of the ratings was not assessed, and that the physiological evidence was slight.

The physiological organs most intimately associated with individual temperament are the endocrine glands. These are situated in various parts of the body and send their secretions directly into the blood-stream. The *thyroid* is situated below the larynx. If it under-functions certain physical features develop and the person tends to become dull and apathetic. Over-functioning tends to produce over-activity and anxiety. The *adrenals* are situated above the kidneys. One of their functions is the secretion of adrenalin, which puts the body into a kind of emergency state, increasing the blood-pressure, relaxing the muscles concerned with digestion and elimination, and causing other physical changes characteristic of fear or anger.

The *pituitary*, at the base of the brain, exercises a controlling influence over physical growth and metabolism and over the other glands. The *gonads*, or sex glands, govern the development of the distinctive superficial differences between male and female bodies, and the various patterns of sexual behaviour. The influences and inter-relations of these and other glands have been extensively studied. The knowledge is too specialized to be of great practical assistance to teachers. Serious abnormalities are matters for medical diagnosis. What is important for the teacher is the realization that there are these powerful physiological agents working in the body and influencing behaviour. The adolescent's quickly developing interest in sexual and social matters is not the product of environmental or intellectual influences alone. The potency of these new interests derives from the radical physiological changes which thrust the child forward into adulthood.

The most scientific typology is based on factorial analysis. A large number of assessments of varied kinds is made of a large number of people. The assessments are correlated and the correlations analysed into factors. This procedure does not make any individual assessment more scientific in itself, but it helps to minimize the number of general personality traits, by showing where a set of apparently varied assessments may be, in fact, measuring the same personality trait. Vernon (1953) mentions two major dimensions of personality which may be completely independent. One is a factor ranging from dependability at one extreme to undependability at the other. The second factor ranges from complete extraversion (an out-going, uninhibited personality) to complete introversion (an inward-turning, inhibited personality). Two such completely independent factors are said to be *orthogonal*—that is, at right angles to one another. If a factor is not completely independent, but is partly correlated with another, it is said to be *oblique*. Represented by a line, an oblique factor makes less than one right angle with its fellows. One of Vernon's oblique factors is 'dominance—submission.' The dominant end of this continuum is closely associated with extraversion, the submissive end with introversion.

Eysenck (1953) refers to a personality model with three orthogonal or independent factors. 'Extraversion—introversion' is the same as in Vernon. A factor called 'neuroticism' is rather like Vernon's 'dependability—undependability.' But Eysenck adds a factor called 'psychoticism' which he, unlike some writers, differentiates from neuroticism. Psychoticism would run from a tendency to develop the mental illness called a psychosis to a tendency not to be liable to such illness.

With more or less reliability, a person can be allotted to his correct position on each factorial continuum. Our hypothetical average man would stand at the centre of the system, equally balanced between extraversion and introversion, dependability and undependability, proneness to and freedom from psychotic tendencies. The more a person is sensitive, seclusive, nervous, given to inferiority feelings and the like, the more he lies towards the pole of introversion. The more he is 'thick-skinned,' sociable, cheerful, and confident, the more he approximates to the extraversion pole. His placing on the continuum of neuroticism or 'dependability—undependability' would be determined by how far he manifests emotional stability, freedom from apprehensiveness, independence, good physical health, ability to achieve happy social and personal adjustments, or the opposites of these.

While this factorial typology leaves many questions to be answered, the use of continua instead of entirely distinct classes permits it to accommodate subtle differences of individual personality within a simple general framework. This answers the charge sometimes uttered, that such systematic analyses are bound in some way to destroy the uniqueness of personality. A teacher, having such a framework in mind, would modify his attitudes, methods, and advice, according to whether he was dealing with a child near the centre of the framework (and such children would be the majority), or one whose emotional instability required sympathetic and firm guidance towards independence, or one whose out-going exuberance needed good-humoured but firm restraint. But he would have to remember that the framework is sketchy and does not take account of the complications of intellectual and environmental variations, which may masquerade as temperament or transmogrify genuine temperamental factors almost beyond recognition. He would also remember that these complicated variations of personality are needed for the varied purposes of life, and that none is ideal in every sense.

Many devices are used in the assessment of personality :

(1) Paper and pencil tests may require the person to say what he would do in various personality-revealing situations, or to list activities that he likes or dislikes, or things that please or worry him.

(2) A certain response called the 'psychogalvanic skin response' (PGR) may be measured to indicate different degrees of response in different kinds of laboratory situations.

(3) Real-life situations may be devised in which the person has to participate while observers assess his behaviour. This has been used in the selection both of officers during war-time and of senior civil servants in time of peace.

(4) Information or personal assessments may be given by those who know an individual well, or, as in many interviews, by those who rely on their own 'spot' judgments based on general acquaintance with people.

(5) Projection tests may be used in which a person reads his own meaning into vague and unstructured stimuli, such as ink-blots or indeterminate pictures which can be interpreted in many ways.

These devices are interesting and have been extensively studied. Unfortunately, none of them has proved to be as statistically reliable or valid as the best intellectual tests. Often those methods that seem most fair and reasonable to the persons assessed have the lowest correlations with later criteria. Interviewing, for example, despite its widespread use and the high valuation popularly placed on it, has been repeatedly shown to have little association with later success and failure. In some cases the inclusion of an interview assessment among others has actually reduced the correlation. A few tests and items of information have sometimes correlated more highly with later success and failure than more elaborate predictive procedures. In defence of the interview, we should recall that the procedure is sometimes used when the candidates are already highly selected, and of similarly high ability. The final choice has to be one of personal judgment, and this may be all to the good if the successful candidate has to work with his interviewers, or in their interests. Vernon (1953) makes the further points that the validity of the interview may be lowered more than the validity of tests by failure to follow up the rejected candidates; and that the interview may be compared with the *best* of several tests, or with a group of tests that have been statistically weighted to give their highest possible validity. (For example, instead of taking the simple total of three test scores, a better prediction might be given by adding half of score one, the whole of score two, and twice score three.)

There is an immense literature on projection tests. It has been claimed that the Rorschach ink-blots can be used to assess the intellectual as well as the emotional aspect of personality. The administration and interpretation of such tests are skilled and time-consuming procedures. They cannot be used on a large scale, although attempts have been made to adapt them. Attention is paid to the number and kind of responses made by a person, to the shapes and colours that guide his responses, and to the balance between responses to details and to more general aspects of the ink-blot. Where pictures are used, as in the Thematic Apperception Test, the aim is to encourage the expression of those personal themes which concern the individual at the deeper levels of personality. Again interpretation is a somewhat equivocal matter, and statistical reliabilities and validities are not high.

The device that is of commonest concern to a teacher is the personality rating. Ratings cannot be avoided in one form or another. Although they too are most imperfect, psychologists have pointed out certain features that were not fully appreciated in the past and the recognition of which can improve this type of personality assessment in practice. Firstly, it has been shown repeatedly that a 'halo effect' operates in ratings. In other words, if a child impresses the teacher favourably in one respect the teacher is liable to give him a halo which may irradiate other qualities too favourably. The safeguard is to make deliberately independent assessments of separate qualities or, better still, have the assessments made by independent persons who know different aspects of the child's personality. This is not easy in school situations, for information spreads so quickly and stereotyped judgments are readily established.

Secondly, it has been shown that teachers' ratings tend to be distributed differently from what psychologists prefer. Vernon (1953) illustrates this in the case of a five-point scale. The percentage distribution preferred by the psychologist, and that commonly found, are as follows :

	A	B	C	D	E
Preferred by psychologists	7	24	38	24	7
Commonly found	3	60	30	7	0

Teachers are reluctant to award top marks to too many children lest they should be encouraged to slack off in their work; and to give too many low marks lest the poorer children should be discouraged or the class average seem too poor. This shows how assessments are often used for purposes other than summing up a person's achievement. In assessing general personality traits, there is a desire to avoid stigmatizing many with a low assessment or apparently favouring many with a high assessment. In some classes, of course, the range of ability or personality may be genuinely narrow. The psychologist's normal distribution presumes a population that has not been already selected for the trait in question.

Thirdly, unsatisfactory ratings sometimes emerge because there has been insufficient definition of what is wanted, insufficient discussion of the nature of personality traits, and insufficient evidence that the ratings will serve any practical purpose. The first two shortcomings show again how important it is that teachers should learn to understand personality in a wide sense, and not in a narrow, rule-of-thumb manner. If ratings are carelessly made because they are not put to practical use the solution is to stop wasting time by making such ratings.

Fourthly, either the teacher or the person who requires him to make ratings sometimes assumes that it is enough to have a rating scale such as the following on which a cross can be marked.

—————————————X————————————————————

| Extremely | Very | Confident | Rather | Extreme lack |
| confident | confident | | timid | of confidence |

Alternatively, it is enough to put down a letter rating from

A to E. But often some piece of concrete information is as useful as a general rating. If this is so the information should be recorded, or communicated to whom it will be of use. Again, it can be seen that there is futility in recording only general assessments if something else provides the real practical clue to a child's needs.

Fifthly, teachers should think of their ratings as being limited to a child as they know him. In the past there has been some tendency to think of personality traits as being fixed, unalterable, or even innate. A more accurate view would be that certain relatively stable personality traits can be detected by the teacher, but that a child's behaviour in situations unknown to the teacher may manifest a radically different personality.

Ratings, like typologies, represent an attempt to *sum up* personality. The study of glandular balances or other physiological functions represents an attempt to penetrate the physical depths of personality. The psychoanalytic movements stemming from Freud represent the most influential endeavour to penetrate the *psychological depths* of personality. The central assertion is that much of an individual's behaviour is determined by subconscious parts of his personality (that is, by processes of which all of us are unconscious for some of the time). Speaking in the metaphorical manner of psychoanalysts, we should say that the unconscious is the abode of the *id*, the instinctive drives towards creation (especially through sexual activity) and destruction (ultimately to the point of death). The *id* shares the unconscious with the *super-ego*, which is the ideal of himself which each person unconsciously builds up under the influence of his earliest education. This ideal embodies particularly his private conception of the rôles played by his mother and father. The *ego* is the conscious aspect of personality, which observes the world and reasons about it, and achieves a greater or lesser harmony over the turbulent and eruptive world of the unconscious.

This vivid picture of human personality can be criticized for giving an unwarranted substantiality to features of human behaviour that could be described in a common-sense way. Such a criticism need not detract from the illumination shed by psychoanalytic ideas. There is no doubt that people are deeply influenced by impulses of which they are often unaware, and by past experiences which they have forgotten to the extent of disowning them. The evidence for this is varied. Common observation provides many examples of people failing to recognize influences which are only too obvious to their friends—the forgetting of promises that a person does not really want to fulfil or of knowledge that does not really interest him, the projection of blame for disappointments on to any person or thing other than oneself, and the persistence in adult life of forms of adjustment which originated in childhood. Psychoanalytic studies have suggested that there are various media, such as dreams and the free association of ideas, which can help a person to become aware of things in himself of which he has been unconscious. Different forms of psychotherapy have been based on these or similar ideas.

This conception of personality gives a prominent place to the earliest years of life. It is argued that the infant's experience of security and satisfaction, and the availability of parents who embody good but realistic standards of living, determine the child's later development to a great extent. A child whose parents expect too much too early (often beginning with precocious toilet-training) may grow up with combined feelings of hostility and anxiety. An over-indulged child will not be realistic enough and will, therefore, have trouble when others prove less indulgent than his parents. Where such indulgence represents an attempt to compensate with material rewards for lack of genuine parental feeling for the child, he may also develop anxiety or hostility. In one version the child's infantile development has three critical phases—the *oral*, derived from the earliest feeding experiences, in which the child's interest is focused on his mouth; the *anal*, derived from toilet-experience, in which the child is interested in excretory processes; and the *erotic*, in which the child discovers the sensuous possibilities of his body, and especially of the sexual organs. Unsatisfactory experience of any of those stages might result in a fixation at that stage, and in an impediment to later development of the personality. The existence of these phenomena in some form seems sufficiently substantiated, but there is little satisfactory evidence about the implications for later personality development.

Various elements have been stressed by different analytic psychologists. Freud stressed the pre-eminence of sexual development even at the infantile stage. Jung expounded his curious belief in the organic inheritance of some psychic knowledge, a kind of racial inheritance of the conceptions (archetypes) found in the world's great myths. Adler emphasized feelings of inferiority or superiority, and man's will to power. A much-refined theory is associated with the American psychiatrist Adolf Meyers. Behaviour is thought to be a psychobiological expression of the whole organism. It is shaped by the individual's constitution and by his general pattern of development. It has many determinants. Psychotherapy, therefore, should not be restricted by any single theory. The modern trend towards combining the case material and psychological processes discussed by the earlier psychoanalysts with the behavioural or biological outlook of many American psychologists seems to be a sensible one.

The Meyers point of view, well expounded by Masserman (1946), is a revolt against the hide-bound categories of the past. Another and partly similar approach to general psychology is associated with the name of Lewin (1954). His topological psychology rejects the sharp division between the personality and the physical environment. He puts forward the concept of the *biosphere*. Formidable as this seems, it signifies only the person and his environment considered as one entity. This is intended to emphasize the

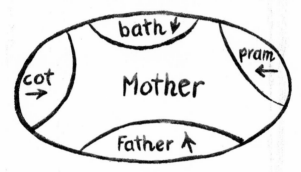

Fig. 7. A SIMPLE BIOSPHERE

oneness of the psychological world, and the fact that what matters psychologically is the world as it exists for the person in question. A baby would have a simple biosphere of the kind illustrated. In many situations the prevalent field of force would be one moving the baby towards the mother. As the baby developed, the biosphere would be differentiated into more complex areas and forces. Mother might lose some of her positive attraction, and the resultant forces would more often send the child in father's direction. All kinds of pulls and conflicts can be represented until the biosphere has a marvellous complexity. Whether it will ever represent more than an interesting illustrative technique is not clear.

This brief review of various general approaches to personality clears the ground for a closer study of the development of children from infancy to adulthood, and subsequently for a fuller exploration of unconscious processes, and of mental health in relation to the problems of children and teachers.

Chapter Ten

Infancy and Childhood

I T is understandable and right that teachers should attach importance to the influence of schools in educating young people, but many of the problems and limitations that confront a teacher have their origin in the pre-school period. Studies of pre-school, and indeed of pre-natal, development shed illumination on these problems and limitations, and also on the nature of growth, maturation, or development.

When a single male sex cell fertilizes a single female sex cell the inheritance of the future child is already laid down. The resulting zygote, as it is called, has forty-six chromosomes, twenty-three from each parent cell. These chromosomes, or the genes which constitute them, are the particles that carry heritable qualities. The zygote now divides into two cells, and each of these into two more, and so on until a recognizable human embryo is in existence. As time goes on the specialized organs of the body become distinct. The process of maturation before and after birth is a continuous one. The new-born baby is in many ways as helpless as one not yet born. The continuity of the maturation process is important educationally, for many things cannot be taught to a child before he has achieved the relevant kind and degree of maturity. Along with this it must be recognized that a child may reach a certain level of physical and mental maturation, and fail in a task for lack of stimulation and encouragement to realize his potentialities.

The newly born baby is dependent above all on the good care of a mother or a foster-mother. The need for constant physical care is obvious, but it is only more recently that such emphasis has been laid on the affectionate quality of the care. Babies brought up institutionally may have the most scrupulous physical care from a purely hygienic point of view, and yet develop more slowly than children reared by their own mothers or by good individual foster-mothers. As in later human relationships, the qualities of genuineness or sincerity and of stability seem to be prerequisites of development. Even in adult relationships physical proximity and contact are important in sustaining such sentiments. In the case of babies the medium of physical contact, especially in the vital feeding situation, is all-important. A better example could hardly be found of how the physical and the psychological interact.

A child's first and most influential educator is his mother or foster-mother. She, by her own personality and associated manner of child-rearing, will establish a sense of security or insecurity, stability or instability, adventure or caution, assertion or submission, confidence or guilt. The father will contribute his influence, at first indirectly through his own relationship with the mother, later more directly in his examples of co-operation with or divergence from the mother in the conduct of daily life. The infant not only develops outwardly according to how his parents treat him, but also takes over the conceptions of conduct that seem to him implicit in such treatment. He is too young to incorporate such conceptions in a highly intellectual form; they are absorbed with a degree of distortion and imperfection analogous to an adult's perception of some radically new and emotionally charged situation. The fact that an infant learns only gradually to distinguish himself as a separate part of the world facilitates the confusion within him of notions that seem quite distinct to adults.

When children first come to school at 5 or 6 years of age their ways of looking at the world and of responding to people and problems are already far developed. They vary widely in respect of physical inheritance. They vary widely in respect of the psychological factors which have just been mentioned. And, more obviously, they vary in the superficial but important cultural and material advantages and disadvantages of different kinds of home. The recognition of such vast differences is a prerequisite of good infant-class education. In later classes the spread of achievement among children tends to become still wider. This prevents any simple general programme of education for all. Teachers have to study the varying needs of their pupils and construct a correspondingly varied programme, having regard to what is practicable in any given circumstances.

Gesell (1954) distinguishes five principles of infantile development which are interesting in themselves and as an indication of what development means :

(1) The principle of *developmental direction* refers to the fact that children mature in certain directions rather than others. The order of development of motor functions, for example, is from head to foot and from the centre of the body to the periphery. The baby gains control of its head and arm muscles (4 to 7 months) before its trunk and hand muscles (7 to 10 months). It is only between 10 months and 1 year that forefinger and thumb come under control, enabling baby to poke and pluck. Similarly, the eye can follow horizontal movement before vertical, and vertical before circular; the child can draw a circle before a square, and a square before a diamond; he can walk upstairs before downstairs; he can perceive differences between objects before he can perceive similarities; he defines an object by its purpose (a chair is to sit on) before

he classifies it more abstractly (an article of furniture). The actual time of reaching these developmental stages varies immensely from child to child, but the order of develop ment is constant.

(2) The principle of *reciprocal interweaving* refers to the complexity of the strands of growth that have to weave themselves together to establish any major function. Gesell distinguishes twenty-three stages in the development of upright posture during the first year of life. There are alternating periods of dominance by the muscular flexors and extensors until the creature that was once bent in his mother's arms stands erect, extended by his own muscles. The acquisition of reading, counting, and the other scholastic skills requires a similarly prolonged organization of component strands. The process is life-long.

(3) *Functional asymmetry* refers to the fact that human beings are not usually ambidextrous. Either the right limbs and organs or the left tend to be functionally superior. Much study has been made of left-handedness because it is an asymmetry which might handicap a person in a world of machines designed for right-handed people. Recommendations are varied, but one view is that, while all children should be encouraged to use their right hands, a persistent left-handed tendency should not be made a cause of worry and strain. A very early example of asymmetry is the tonic neck reflex (t.n.r.) in young babies. If the baby is lying in a free position on its back it turns its head to the right, with the right arm stretched in the same direction and the left hand held up to the left shoulder, like a fencing stance. Alternatively, the t.n.r. is in a leftward direction, with corresponding positions of the arms.

(4) The principle of *individuating maturation* could be illustrated with Lewin's biosphere. As time passes, the biosphere (the child and his environment) becomes more

and more highly differentiated. Increasingly specialized
functions emerge out of a background of broad general
functions. Gesell emphasizes that these developing functions
anticipate the demands of the environment. The nervous
system, in a sense, grows out to meet the child's approach-
ing needs. Studies of identical twins showed a striking
coincidence in the times of developing certain functions.
Experiments in which one twin was coached in a skill
(such as stair-climbing), and the other not coached, showed
that training had little effect until the necessary natural
growth had taken place. Once the necessary maturation
had occurred training and encouragement could have
more marked effects. This principle of maturational
readiness is most important in learning the three 'R's.' The
pressures of our educational system tend to cause teachers
to do too much too early with the less bright children. A
later start and a more limited and realistic aim might
diminish the problem of backwardness in junior and
secondary schools.

(5) The principle of *regulatory fluctuation* refers to the
fact that children will vary greatly even in relation to
what seems to be their own norms. Gesell refers to studies
of babies who fed or slept according to their own schedules
with the minimum of adult interference. The feeding and
sleeping rhythms fluctuated greatly over a period, but
there was also a pattern of development. A baby who slept
for nineteen hours in his fourth week came round, via a
fluctuating interval, to a period of thirteen hours' sleep in
his fortieth week. Gesell thinks of this aspect of development as a spiral. The child goes forward and back over
short periods, but there is a steady rising to new heights.
This too is a phenomenon that becomes familiar to the
teacher. Its recognition will make him more tolerant of
temporary halts or even regressions in children's learning.

While children live as whole unitary organisms, it is

necessary to distinguish different aspects of their development for the purposes of analytic study. Gesell uses the four
categories of motor development, adaptive development,
language development, and personal-social development.
Motor development refers to physical movement and
co-ordination. Adaptive development refers to the child's
initiation of new experiences and learning from old experiences. The scope of each category has been further defined
in terms of a number of behaviour situations. The details
of these and typical patterns of development are given in
Gesell's books. Another common set of categories is that
of the physical, emotional, social, and intellectual aspects
of behaviour and growth. For the purpose of the present
chapter, some aspects of childhood that most concern
teachers will be selected for special comment.

The development of language in children is equally
interesting to mothers and teachers. During the first 2
months of life a baby makes various vocal sounds. Between
2 and 4 months he responds to the human voice. Between
4 and 8 months his vocalizations may express pleasure or
recognition. Between 8 and 9 months he listens to familiar
words. Between 9 months and 1 year he responds to gestures
or to "bye-bye." During the second year he begins to have
a vocabulary. In the second half of the year he names
single objects and pictures, and responds to questions.
Towards the end of the year he begins to combine words. At
first, words are used in a very general sense. Any man may
be "Da-da." Naming precedes the use of verbs and
adjectives. Relationships come later. Only the most
advanced children are using pronouns at the end of the
second year. At 18 months single words have the force of
sentences. Sentence length slowly increases to about seven
words at the age of 7. The timing of this developmental
pattern varies greatly, but there is a moral in the observation that, even in the relatively rapid period of infantile

growth, language advances at a slow, gradual pace. During the primary-school years it is too easy to become impatient with this quality of language development. The student struggling with the problems of essay-writing, the graduate battling with a Ph.D. thesis, and the teacher writing a letter of application, ought to have considerable sympathy with the six-year-old's attempts to read or the eleven-year-old's difficulties with language usage.

The influence of environment on language development is well-recognized. Children reared in institutions tend to be retarded. Children from families of high socio-economic status tend to be advanced. Children whose family life has a well-developed social quality have an advantage. The language of only children tends to be developed by conversation with their parents rather than with siblings. Girls tend to be in advance of boys in all aspects of language development; this may be associated with their advancement in social interests and relationships. Teachers will take all these generalizations into account in planning their programme. At whatever level they are able to pitch the work, it is important (a) to provide plenty of concrete or pictorial illustration to support language development, (b) to provide plenty of opportunities for talking about things as a preparation for the more exacting task of writing, and (c) to make full use of what children already know or are interested in.

As play is one of the main interests of children at all ages, much attention has been given to this activity. Many theories have been expounded. Features of play that have been emphasized include (a) its capacity to provide an outlet for 'surplus energy,' (b) its alleged recapitulation of the history of the race (little boys emulating monkeys!), (c) its value in preparing the young for adult life (exercise of physical, social, and competitive skills), (d) its frequently imitative quality (playing at schools, shops, hospitals, etc.),

(e) its voluntary quality, as distinct from tasks imposed as work, (f) its similarity to art in respect of spontaneous joy and self-discipline, and (g) its frequent quality of make-believe or fantasy with obvious or more recondite symbolizations of real-life situations and problems. Each of these provides an interesting point of discussion, but the last three are most directly relevant to education.

The fact that children will put a great deal of hard work into an activity that they regard as play has given rise to the play-way in education. The success of this as a teaching method depends on the teacher's subtlety and sincerity more than on the method alone. The children may play without achieving any of the distinctive purposes for which educational systems are established; or the play may be directed in a manner which shows the children that they are not really playing. As in so many educational situations, no system will compensate for the absence of sincerity. The teacher's whole attitude to children may have something of the quality of their own leaders' attitudes in play. The legitimacy and desirability of being given a lead is accepted, but the leader must not become domineering and turn voluntary effort into a compulsory imposition.

Adults, by their greater emotional and linguistic maturity, are enabled to discuss their personal problems with others, or reflect upon them analytically. But even they handle such problems in less intellectual ways, imagining themselves into hypothetical situations that might follow upon different decisions, going over the problems in strangely distorted forms as in their recollections of dreams. Children are still more poorly equipped to work out their personal problems at an intellectual level. Much of their play represents a kind of reflection upon the world and themselves in terms of concrete objects and actual activities. An adult who has had some new experience will tell his story over and over again, making it a familiar part of his personality both to himself and others. The repetitive and imitative play of children serves a similar function. Children who have had more than the normal experience of hospitals have been observed to play at hospitals more often than usual. A child who experienced a death in the family spent some time making a great number of "Plasticine" coffins. Play is a way of coming to terms with the world and, where some problem presses sorely upon the child's spirit, of discharging the pent-up emotion. The psychologist tends to be more concerned about the child who has difficulty in purging his feelings than about the child who wreaks havoc on his toy armies or wooden blocks.

The joke about father monopolizing junior's electric train points to a genuinely important psychological consideration. Adults may buy toys to please themselves and, worse still, force adult conceptions of handling toys on children. Psychologists would favour a variety of playthings for children, including especially such uncostly items as old boxes, shells, pieces of string, cloth, paper, and all those things the use of which can be infinitely varied. In the psychological clinic representative toys (dolls, houses, etc.) are available to enable a child to symbolize his own world, but also inchoate material such as sand, clay, dough, or water, which, because of their relative freedom from conventional significance, give wider scope to the child's fantasy. The observation of play can help to diagnose children's personal problems. The opportunity to play can help them to make their problems more tolerable. Play is both diagnostic and therapeutic.

The principles of child-development which have been discussed in this chapter have been recognized and applied most extensively in the realm of children under 7 years of age. This is so partly because infants are more available

for study, partly because they are not exposed to the
rigours of a full scholastic curriculum, and partly because
their behaviour is less sophisticated or inhibited. Between
the ages of 7 and 11, however, the opposite conditions
tend to prevail. This period is one of slow, steady growth
as contrasted with the relatively rapid development of
infancy. The differences between the two periods may
cause primary-school teachers to feel that the principles
discussed in this chapter do not apply at all to their work,
especially in view of the strong pressures to achieve
scholastic progress. Scholastic success is certainly one of
the main aims of the primary school, but even this may
be impeded by a disregard for the total pattern of children's
development. It may, therefore, be worth while outlining
a policy of compromise between the claims of examinations and the claims of general education in primary
schools.

Primary-school teachers, like others, have to consider
what might be called the economics of their teaching
methods. Just as it has been found that excessive working
hours in industry may not increase, but rather decrease,
the rate of production, so excessive concentration on one
aspect of primary-school work may be deleterious. The
teacher and other educators have to work out a balance
between the various parts of the curriculum. Tests and
observation must be used to determine appropriate levels
and rates of work. Examination achievements must not be
the outcome of forced labour, evaporating as soon as the
pressures are relaxed. If a child must get a low mark is he
not better to get his 25 per cent. (let us say) for doing one
question well rather than for doing several poorly? The
teacher has an individual opportunity and responsibility
not only for preserving children from improper examination tensions, but for maintaining those humane educational ideals which are not measured by examination

results. When the teacher has used all his skill to facilitate a child's total educational progress there should be no recriminations on account of any final shortcomings. More general understanding of child development and more techniques of using the understanding are available than ever before, but they still have to be embodied in the teacher's own mind and practice.

The psychological study of children is closely associated with the philosophy of 'naturalism,' because it stresses the importance of the 'natural' or unforced growth of children. The other main educational philosophy has been called 'idealism,' because it stresses the importance of cultivating children deliberately towards various adult ideals. The psychologist can only map certain outlines suggested by his survey of the field; he cannot prove the logical necessity of a particular kind of education. The idealist may prove that a particular kind of education is the logical outcome of his general philosophic beliefs, but such an education may be quite impracticable because of its remoteness from the lives of children. In the twentieth century the naturalists have been in the ascendant. More recently it has begun to be appreciated that the natural development of children is so intimately interwoven with the ideals of the society in which they live that the two must be considered together. The teacher alone can work the relationship into school practice and into the lives of the children.

Chapter Eleven

Adolescence and Maturity

ADOLESCENCE is the period between childhood and maturity. It might be considered to begin just before puberty, the time when the sexual organs become functionally active, but there is no simple criterion of reaching adulthood. The law decrees that 21 years of age should be the conventional borderline, but many have fought and died for their countries before that age, and others in ripe middle-age behave in ways more typical of 'teen-agers.' Adolescence provides a particularly interesting study in the ferment of biological and cultural elements. The basis of adolescent growth is physiological—the rapid asynchronous bodily growth together with the relatively dramatic onset of adult sexual functioning. This growth creates problems mainly in relation to the conditions of the society in which it occurs. In Western society the adolescent is thrust, physiologically and psychologically, towards adulthood, but lacks the developed social knowledge and skill, the economic independence, and the self-confidence, to enter completely into the beckoning adult rôle. Even within Western society there are striking national and class differences. In the United States girls and boys 'date' one another earlier than in the United Kingdom. Children who leave school early to start work are in some ways hastened towards adulthood more than those who stay on at school or college. The facts and problems of adolescence are most obviously the concern of secondary-school teachers, but every person working with children should study the whole pattern of their development. No stage can be isolated in practice or at the deeper levels of psychological understanding.

Charts of the general physical development of children show the most rapid growth during the first year of life. Average height increases from about twenty inches at birth to about twenty-eight inches at 1 year. Weight increases from eight or nine pounds to about twenty-two pounds. These increases of 40 and 150 per cent. respectively in 1 year may be compared with corresponding increases of only 25 and 100 per cent in the 9 years of adolescent growth. Development up to the age of 20 continues fairly steadily and steeply. About the age of 11, at an average height of about fifty-two inches and weight of about sixty-six pounds, the girls begin to surpass the boys; but, by the age of 13 or 14, the boys retrieve their superiority in these dimensions, and go on to higher adult averages.

Kuhlen (1952) quotes the average age of girls at the menarche as about 13, with a range from 10 to 18, or possibly wider. Kinsey (1948) gives the average age of the first male orgasm resulting in the ejaculation of semen as 13 years 10 months, with a range from 8 to 21. These two events differ in that the first is a physiological preparation for later possible child-bearing, while the second is itself a physical arousal of a sexual nature. The onset of puberty tends to be earlier in girls, but the nature of the onset in boys represents a more advanced physiological-sexual status. Physiologically, boys have more and earlier sexual experience and are stimulated by a wider variety of situations. Socially, girls are more advanced in their sexual interests. The Freudian view that boys and girls pass through a homosexual phase of attachment to friends of the same sex is rejected by Kinsey, who found in the United States that large proportions of men and women have experienced no homosexual response. Freud was thinking, no doubt, of the partial psychological-social segregation of the sexes which is an observable feature of the early teens, while Kinsey was referring to physiological responses. Freud's society segregated the sexes more than does the modern American society described by Kinsey. Girls do tend, more than boys, to have emotional attachments to older members of their own sex, but such 'crushes' are also commoner where the girls are segregated in the single-sex society of a girls' boarding school. Similarly, boys' boarding schools are more likely to encourage comparable male attachments. Such phases are generally temporary provided there are sympathetic and understanding adults.

Physical appearance is of great concern to adolescents. To be healthy and well-proportioned and attractive helps greatly in developing social relationships. Any shortcoming or imagined shortcoming in these areas is important, not so much in itself as in its psychological effect. Young people learn gradually to value qualities other than superficial appearance, but physique is the most obvious manifestation of development. The youth who develops a mature appearance at an early age tends to be given mature status sooner than the one who, perhaps in his late teens, is still small in size or under-developed, or otherwise lacking in the physical signs of maturity. These facts constitute a further warning of the danger of assuming that apparent personality is insusceptible of change.

Adolescence has been represented as a period of emotional stress. More recently this conception has been criticized. Kuhlen suggests that adolescent stress may really be parental stress caused by adolescents; that the vagaries of adolescence emerge only when the characters of diverse individuals are merged into a composite idea; and that genuine stresses and vacillations are no more marked than in comparable persons at other ages. Adolescence, like all growth, is gradual, total, and complex; not sudden, fragmentary, and dramatically simple. The important points of reference are (a) social adjustment towards independence from parents and co-operation with young people of the opposite sex; (b) preparation for vocational and economic independence; and (c) ideological development towards a personal philosophy or religion.

The emotional quality of adolescence is presumably determined by the smoothness with which these various developments are completed. In England 85 per cent. of boys and girls leave school at 15 (1951 census). Only a minority enter apprenticeship or receive organized training. Generally glad to cast off scholastic restraints, they are quite speedily absorbed into the adult workaday world of sports, television, cinemas, dancing, picture magazines, annual holidays, smoking, visiting, lounging, strolling, courting, and getting married. Dispersed in all their workshops, offices, and stores, inaccessible to psychological researchers, started on the path of economic and therefore of personal freedom, this vast majority of adolescents has perhaps contributed too little to the composite picture of adolescence, compared with the minority in school and college. The adolescent majority is criticized for its intellectual poverty or its pursuit of vulgarity, triviality, and escape. Some blame the schools. Others, more constructively, are suggesting that we have yet to take a close look at the adolescent worker's emotional problems, and work out schemes of guidance and training for work and for leisure. The *Citizens of Tomorrow* report (1955) recommends "that the training of teachers should be broadened to include substantial understanding of working conditions." The impermanence of the effects of ten years' schooling suggests that the content and methods of the past need to be revised in the direction of something more deeply cultural, that is, of values which enrich the lives of

the young but which are related to the psychological
realities of these lives.

Gesell (1956) portrays adolescence as an alternation
between balanced expressive phases and rather tense
reflective phases, with a slow improvement in all-round
adjustment. The ten-year-old is contented, casual, fond of
his home, his school, his play, and his physical activities.
The eleven-year-old is more turbulent; he is restive, argu-
mentative, even dramatically rude, but also curious and
eager. The twelve-year-old is positive, enthusiastic, and
spirited. The thirteen-year-old is reflective and self-
absorbed, critical of himself and of others. The fourteen-
year-old is friendly, co-operative, and interested in people.
The fifteen-year-old passes through a period of relatively
high tension; he is now apathetic, now gregarious, and
always increasingly desirous of independence. The sixteen-
year-old is self-assured, cheerful, tolerant, and mindful
of people. Boys tend to be more interested in the scientific,
outdoor, and sporting aspects of the world : girls in indoor
recreations, and in the personal, social, and ethical aspects.
All this is but a general characterization, requiring more
substantiation than is yet available. It is not a set of
developmental norms, but a suggestion of the broad
pattern of adolescent development.

Adolescent emotions can be intense and variable and
imperfectly controlled. Bitterness or joy may arise from
failure or success, especially in the realms of independence
from parental restrictions, of employment or study, and
of social and sexual relationships. Intellectual doubts and
anxieties can also have a strongly emotional tone. Some
emotions may be refined and directed into sentiments of
patriotism, devoutness, or altruism. Others may momen-
tarily run wild as half-rational fears or angers. These
characteristics may not be distinctive of adolescence, but

adolescence is a period when they are least susceptible of being overlooked by adults.

The adolescent is happy in a crowd of his peers, talking, playing, and eating with them in informal circumstances. Hurlock (1949) suggests a large number of purposes that may be served by this lively social life. It offers security and pleasure, and the opportunity of learning to get along with people, to develop tolerance, to acquire social skills, to experience courtship behaviour, and to develop loyalty. On the other hand, it may lead to the neglect of other responsibilities, to group snobbishness, and to misery for those individuals who are excluded. The factors which may isolate an adolescent from group membership are unattractiveness, physical handicap, marked difference from others, geographic isolation, insecurity, self-absorption, a domineering character, over-modesty, snobbishness, quarrelsomeness, being too stupid or too clever, having little in common with the group, or having parents who will not tolerate its members. The opposite qualities would make for successful group membership or leadership. Some of these factors are controllable, and circumstances can be arranged to give an adolescent a good chance socially.

The activities and values of an adolescent group are sometimes called the adolescent 'peer culture,' in so far as they represent a direct influence upon, and point of reference for, an individual adolescent. The peer culture is a half-way house between doing what parents ordain and acting independently as a mature adult. It reflects the realities of adolescent psychology by its very nature, whereas parents often act on assumptions appropriate to earlier childhood. The peer culture provides a forum for self-assertion, tempered by the necessary discipline of conformity to group values. Intellectual, athletic, social, or religious leaders emerge and may influence their fellows deeply. Smaller cliques may exist within a wider group, and intimate individual friendships are struck up which may last for quite long periods. With the necessary social and linguistic means at his disposal, the adolescent is more able to express his problems in words rather than through the symbolic play of childhood. Every topic under the sun is thrashed out in long discussions and arguments.

As the adolescent is drawn away from home into the society of his equals, parents are liable to feel aggrieved. The relatively settled assumptions of years are questioned or rejected. Daughter would rather go with her friend to the cinema than stay at home with mother. Son comes home late, to father's annoyance. Neither is now so keen to go places with mother and father if friends of his or her own age have another plan afoot. The adolescent may admire and love his parents and at the same time resent the restrictions, guilt-feelings, and anxieties which they impose. The parents too love their child but resent his growing away from them. The more parents and children have become tied to one another, the more difficult adolescence is liable to be. Mutual criticism and suspicion may persist until the young person's break-away is complete enough to command recognition, or, less happily, until he submits to the bonds of home and postpones his own maturity. Where parental love has maintained some element of detachment and adults have found satisfaction in their own generation, the adolescent has an easier and healthier path to maturity. It is not suggested that the absence of conflict between the generations is either desirable or practicable. Such absence might hinder maturity by taking away any challenge to self-development.

Some social psychologists, in enthusiasm for their subject, would almost discard the idea of individual psychology and explain all behaviour in terms of group memberships and references. The individual would become the centre of gravity of a great number of inter-penetrating social spheres. The adolescent would, for example, be explained in terms of family, peer culture, friendships; school, work, and recreation groups; religious, political, and social affiliations. While these may be relatively objective, it would be necessary to add imaginative associations, such as the worlds of the cinema, which are (at least temporarily) as psychologically real in their excitement, wealth, glamour, power, sentiment, and adventure. There is no doubt that much of a person's apparent individuality can be analysed into ideas and practices adopted, consciously or unconsciously, from the many groups of which he is a member. But the elements are not simply added one to another; they are compounded in such variety that the approach of individual psychology is a necessary complement to that of social psychology.

Intellectual development of the kind measured by school tests of intelligence seems to stop in the middle of the adolescent period, but, in a wider sense, intellectual development goes on into adulthood. It is during adolescence that the great problems of life are most intensely felt and debated. For the less intellectual they pose themselves in terms of work, marriage, birth, and religious practice. For the more intellectual the general problems of theology, philosophy, ethics, and politics may give further exciting or agonizing concern. Those who would eschew such matters find themselves thrust willy-nilly before them in the joys and despairs and catastrophes of private and public life. The adolescent intelligence exercises itself not only in philosophic ponderings but in rich outpourings of creative activity, from poetry and drama and social service to the latest crazes in music and dancing. For the adolescent these creations are his own, even if adults comment sourly on their shortcomings or precedents. The scholastic content of intellectual development is sadly evanescent. Even before he leaves school the youth in the less academic stream is often losing some of his hard-won skills in parts of the three 'R's.' Away from school and its daily pressures unused knowledge proves volatile in the extreme. Only the knowledge and skills rewarded in employment or in recreation are reinforced sufficiently to keep them alive.

As the adolescent's intelligence test performance reaches its maximum, as his knowledge of the world steadily expands and he becomes increasingly aware of himself and his powers, it is not surprising that there should be revaluations of the kind mentioned in the preceding paragraph. Earlier conceptions now seem childish, the world is reviewed more independently, and new friends reveal a variety of previously unconsidered viewpoints. The more intelligent the adolescent, the more he needs to establish a comprehensive and realistic philosophy different from the world-picture of childhood. In this intellectual adaptation, already discussed, adults have a valuable part to play. They may be too late in discarding childish models or too precipitate in foisting poorly selected parts of the adult model on young people. For example, they may fail to replace the child's pictorial God with the more abstract conception which alone will satisfy mental maturity. Erring in the opposite direction, they may prescribe 'good' literature which adults feel they themselves ought to read but rarely do. The only adult who can supply just what the adolescent needs, with sufficient variety and with subtlety of timing, is he who himself knows the problems as live and open issues.

Some of the criticisms vented upon adolescents reflect the dead and imperceptive minds of those who make them. The adolescent needs help rather than criticism. This is well exemplified in the sphere of vocational choice, where young people leaving school at 15, and others continuing through the school to the university, may choose jobs and courses on trivial or irrelevant grounds. The adolescent may aspire beyond his capacities. Many feel called but few are chosen for the posts that seem to have high prestige. Sympathetic guidance towards realism is required.

The idea of adult maturity is not a precise one, but one of its marks is the balance established between self-consideration and consideration for the objective facts of situations. There is self-control without undue inhibition of emotional expression. There is sociability without an unceasing need to be in a crowd or to refer all personal problems to others. There is consistency combined with flexibility. There is recognition and acceptance of personal powers and limitations. The mature adult develops realistic aims and masters the means of achieving them. While committing himself fully to the way of life that seems happiest, he has that element of personal detachment which ensures the possibility of objectivity. And objectivity is, in one word, the essence of adulthood.

Citizens of Tomorrow (1955) comprises four reports on young people—at school, in employment, at leisure, and in the Services. Young people are reported to be often lacking in initiative, self-reliance, and independence. The great majority enter employment where there is no provision for proper training. They have too much pocket-money and too little discipline. The vital influence of parents is often diminished when both mother and father are out working. The need for instruction in matters of sex makes itself evident. Certain aspects of the cinema, television, and the street are criticized for their harmful examples to young people. Recommendations made to counter these influences include the advancing of the minimum school-leaving age to 16, the provision of more schemes of guidance and training for employees, still greater encouragement of youth organizations, and the more forceful inculcation of religious faith. The general

principle underlying these recommendations is that of pro-
longing and controlling the process of growing up so that
young people become better adults. The success of the
principle in practice depends on giving rather than
withholding responsibility, and on guiding rather than
condemning the desires and interests of the young.

The educational problems of adolescence have become
wider in this century, for secondary schools must now
educate a large unacademic majority where formerly their
main problems were those of the academic *élite*. The
United States was quick to adapt curricula and methods
in the interests of prolonged education for the majority.
Traditional subjects and methods were modified or
eliminated, new ones introduced, until Americans themselves say that the pendulum had swung too far, endanger-
ing values that are both traditional and relevant to to-day.
In Scotland, where traditional educational values have
been highly persistent, official reports since the Second World
War have given more prominence to child-centred ideas.
The Scottish Education Department's *Junior Secondary
Education* (1955), for example, emphasizes the following
principles in the education of the less academic majority.
Character and conduct are valued above scholastic
achievement. Consequently, the general atmosphere of a
school is given great importance. The amount of factual
knowledge to be imparted and retained should be mini-
mized, and all work should be relevant to the lives of the
pupils. Project methods are recommended. Classes and
curricula should be varied and flexible. Vocational
preparation should be kept in mind, but attained by means
of a sound general education rather than by specific
training.

In the academic secondary schools (academy, grammar
school, *lycée*, or *Gymnasium*) there has probably been
least enthusiasm for modern educational and psychological

ideas. Such schools have highly specialized aims, sanctioned by long tradition, and highly selected pupils, who can more easily depend on themselves and their homes to satisfy the less academic needs of adolescence. The high adaptability of these children enables them to tolerate the imperfections of the system without too obvious upsets. The practically inevitable success of the best of them sanctions the *status quo*. On the debit side, there have been public complaints of overwork and strain in several European countries. Inquiry among university graduates may reveal quite frequent complaints about lack of adequate guidance in their earlier 'choice' of school curricula. The forced knowledge of the academic programme evaporates only too readily as soon as the examination is over. Five or six years' study of a subject may leave a quite highly intelligent pupil with little *practical* command of it. Even where the validity of these criticisms is admitted, there is strong reluctance to do anything about it. Examinations, the promotion of pupils, and the traditional reputation of the school embalm the formula of the past. It works well enough. A change might tempt Fortune.

In defence of the hide-bound academic school, at any rate in Britain, its positive achievements are high—easily sacrificed and not easily attained—and its teachers do unmeasured services of a more child-centred kind outside the stern walls of the curriculum.

How are the psychological and educational aspects of adolescence to be summed up in a practical way? The point of first importance is that teachers, while presenting the highest values as cogently as they can (namely, in their own example), should let plenty of responsibility and free choice devolve upon the young. It is often better for the young to learn the error (if so it be) of their own ways rather than be protected from imagined precocity. To follow such a policy can be extremely trying for the teacher, and he can err in giving too much freedom, but the ability to devolve responsibility is a test of the teacher's maturity as well as of the pupil's. The second major conclusion is that the teacher can direct the attention of an adolescent to facts and ideas, in life and in literature, which may enrich the youth's practical philosophy and counteract more casual and tawdry influences. It is equally true of adolescence as of infancy and childhood that sensitivity is most intense and lasting where the genuine interests of the young meet with the genuine interests of their teachers.

Chapter Twelve

Mental Health

THE ideas of physical health and illness have long been familiar, but it is mainly during the present century that the ideas of mental health and illness have come into prominence. Only slowly, even in modern times, have the varieties of mental illness been analysed, and more effective and humane treatments substituted for the barbarities of the past. As the aim of actively encouraging physical health has followed on the successes of curative medicine, so mental health has emerged as a positive aim for every one rather than as a matter of treatment for those who have already succumbed psychologically to the pressure of their own problems.

This development is associated with two of the main trends in modern psychology. One is the movement towards regarding people as whole personalities; as children, for example, rather than as pupils only; as men and women rather than as employees only. This has brought with it a special emphasis on the emotional and social aspects of personality, just because these had been relatively neglected. The second trend is the recognition of the fact that human characteristics are not commonly measurable on an all-or-nothing, but rather on a more-or-less, scale. If we look at the extremes of genius and mental defect, or of mental health and insanity, the members of each pair are virtually separate categories. But when the intermediate ranges are explored the limits become indistinct. The normal gradually merges into the abnormal in one direction or another. A similar gradual merging is now evident in respect of the physical and the psychological. Physical and psychological states are closely associated, favourable or unfavourable conditions tending to reinforce themselves; we shrewdly employ two senses of having a 'headache' or a 'pain in the neck.'

Some believe that mental health is such a vital matter educationally that they advocate more attention to its principles in the education of teachers. Not only should teachers study the problems of mental health in children, but they should be helped in practical ways to understand themselves. Many of the practical problems discussed in this book have suggested how the psychological welfare of children depends on the psychological health and understanding of parents and teachers. It is a common cliché that child-guidance means parent-guidance. Morris (1955), discussing "Mental Health in the Classroom," recommends that students preparing for teaching should have plenty of group discussions in circumstances which encourage the uninhibited expression of personal and educational problems. Systematic knowledge would be subordinated to the student's felt needs, emotional and intellectual.

The Freudian view of personality and mental health, briefly outlined in the chapter on "Personality," has been greatly developed and in some ways surpassed. Before tracing this development it may be helpful to recapitulate the Freudian viewpoint by referring to Susan Isaacs' study of *Social Development in Young Children* (1933), and to some of the Freudian 'mechanisms' which are of continuing importance. The Isaacs study refers mainly to the pre-school years and is based on the immediate study of a quite small number of children. To the infant everything appears either good or bad, and privation is felt as frustration. The baby is all *id* and no *ego*. At first his psychological life is dominated by fantasy. In the Freudian view some of these fantasies may have cannibalistic or destructive elements, surprising as this may seem when compared with the "trailing-clouds-of-glory" conception of infancy. Emotions of hostility and aggression alternate with those of anxiety and fear in childhood fantasies. This phenomenon, whereby a single personal problem may show itself in apparently opposite states, is called *ambivalence*. As an infant grows into childhood, hostilities, motivated by the urges for possession and power, and directed towards parents, or strangers, or younger or inferior children, are gradually replaced by friendliness and co-operation. Because the earlier fears and aggressions are thought to be associated with the earliest experiences of feeding, excreting, and sexual exploration, the Freudians attach great importance to the proper handling of these aspects of infant nurture. The main features of proper handling are tolerance and frankness. These prevent the growth of guilt feelings and the repression of problems which are best allowed to come into the open.

Freud and his followers have classified some of the main modes of psychological operation in situations where a person is unaware, or not fully aware, of these operations. All kinds of *fantasy*, including day-dreams and night-dreams, constitute one of the main categories of subconscious activity. The most mature and realistic adult may have extravagant day-dreams of his own, or he may find distraction or enlightenment in fantasies manufactured for him by novelists, dramatists, or film-makers. Whoever provides the fantasy, it serves to satisfy needs or inclinations which cannot be satisfied in other ways. The human imagination can manufacture 'needs' and inclinations on a scale that can be matched only by satisfactions belonging to the same world of imagination. Whatever we achieve in objective reality, there is always a greener grass beckoning us on to the other side of the fence. Fantasy is a method of exploring new possibilities.

People who are denied the satisfaction of elementary needs will be more given to fantasy. Children in their play enter adult, animal, or 'inanimate' rôles, and achieve the feeling of power that is normally denied them. Adolescents, held back from the satisfactions of adult life, day-dream themselves into preposterously wish-fulfilling situations. Hungry adults dream of food, and lovelorn wives return to the romantic fiction of their youth. In these cases the preferred fantasy can give a clue to the strongest under-lying motives. Educators, while aiming at an increasing degree of realism or objectivity, do well to develop a sympathetic understanding of the predominant fantasies of different groups, for these point to sources of motiva-tional power. Motivational power is not, of course, an inborn source which can be tapped when found. One person can create such power in another. The advertiser earns his living by doing this for a commercial end as the teacher does for an educational end.

Fantasy ranges from the scarcely intelligible processes of a psychotic in a mental hospital to the highly realistic imaginings of a person contemplating a certain college course, a career, marriage, or his next summer holiday. The latter person imagines himself into various situations, and may live imaginatively through many of the details of them before making a practical choice. At the level of the highest literary or artistic creation, the product is neither a literal representation of the world nor is it fantastic. Insight may be expressed and communicated which partakes of the power of fantasy without losing the objective sense needed in everyday affairs. The men who have such insight have often undergone psychological or physical stresses, although a bare existence under the eaves is not an inevitable formula for genius.

Dreaming is a form of fantasy that may deserve separate mention, for dreams have always aroused interest, and in this century have been used as one method of studying those psychological processes of which their owner is unconscious. Dreams are particularly appropriate for this purpose, for they occur when the conscious part of the mind is (metaphorically) off guard. It is not always completely off guard, however, and the ideas or desires which would not be admitted during wakefulness may still have to disguise themselves in order to slip through in dreams. This implies that dreams are not always to be taken at their face value, but that they may need to be interpreted. The interpretation can be made only in relation to other facts known about the dreamer. The contents of dreams are symbolic and metaphorical, requiring translation into literal terms before their psychological significance becomes apparent. Different people will have different metaphors, but some symbols and metaphors are common in all dreams just as they are in poetry : women may be symbolized as flowers or fruit, success by an exhilarating advance, failure or anxiety by nightmarish falls. Freud emphasized the symbolization of sexual problems, but this bias is not necessary to perceive that the symbolic function of dreams is akin to the ordinary functioning of the human mind. As with other fantasies, dreams can be madly remote from ordinary life or so close that they almost constitute a continued reflection on the problems of the day-time. Their emotional tone can range from the ecstatic through neutrality to the desperate. They are surreptitious comments on ourselves, certainly amusing in some cases, perhaps salutary in some others. If their occurrence is sometimes initiated by the after-effects of a hearty supper, many psychologists would maintain that no physical stimulus alone accounts for their contents.

Repression in the Freudian sense is not a process of

deliberately suppressing something. It is the process whereby our conscious selves cease to recognize some experience that has occurred. While conscious recognition ceases, the repressed material has nevertheless entered into our make-up. Its influence may be seen by some one for whom the material is not so emotionally charged. It is a testimony to the importance of expression that experiences seem to find some way out of us, even if they are not given a conscious outlet. The person who does not face unpleasant problems or personal shortcomings may be oppressed by a vague sense of guilt and be abnormally critical of other people. This excessive blaming of others would be a symptom of some repressed personal problem. Hypochondria is another emergency outlet for repressed problems. The hypochondriac refers his unrecognized problems, not to other people, but to his own imagined ailments and illness. It has already been suggested that bad classroom behaviour and delinquency are crude outlets for unsolved personal problems. Repressed problems can manifest themselves, too, in organic illness. It is widely recognized that much ordinary illness includes a marked psychological element, and that certain real physical illnesses and allergies are associated with psychological difficulties.

Psychotherapeutic methods vary immensely and can include physical as well as psychological techniques. A central aim in the psychological methods is to make the patient once more aware of the problem that has become repressed, and to educate him towards accepting and solving it. This is a process mainly of emotional education, although an intellectual element is inevitable. Repression is not a response to intellectual problems, however prominent the intellectual façade, but to those emotional problems which prove too unbearable. The aim of releasing repressed material has been opportunistically mistranslated by some into the aim of freely indulging all appetites, allegedly to prevent repression. This is a confusion of repression and suppression. The theory of repression is entirely consistent with the desirability of controlling recognized appetites, which have to be reconciled with social or other legitimate interests.

Regression is the appearance of behaviour appropriate to an earlier stage of development than that at which a person now ought to be. An older unmarried lady may behave with adolescent coyness, a frustrated adult indulge in a juvenile temper-tantrum, or a growing infant regress to bed-wetting or -soiling out of envy for the priority awarded to a new baby. *Rationalization* is the manufacture of reasoned justifications to supplant the true causes of behaviour. This happens, almost irresistibly, not only when people seek to excuse themselves, but when they seek to provide a supporting rationale for a decision that is already made. *Compensation* is the placing of excessive emphasis on the satisfactions of one activity as the result of being excluded from success in another.

Identification, or rôle-taking, is the identifying of oneself with some group, thing, or other person. This operates in many fields, from the family or college to material possessions and the fictitious characters of literature, drama, and films. We take on various rôles, often symbolized by insignia or possessions, and such rôles in turn determine much of our behaviour. *Projection* takes two forms. Personal shortcomings may be projected into others and disowned in oneself, or it may be assumed in a more general way that other people are just like oneself and can, therefore, be assimilated into one's own psychological world.

All such mechanisms, which are so common in healthy people, take more serious forms in those who are mentally ill. There is no precise dividing line, but towards the healthy end of the scale people tend to achieve a reasonably contented life, despite all the trials and tribulations of the world; whereas towards the unhealthy end people have become unhappy and, in differing degrees, unable to cope with the ordinary problems of life. We all know people who may be eccentric, rather nervous, prone to minor ailments, irascible, suspicious, juvenile, excessively anxious, or obsessionally tidy; but, fortunately for all of us, we learn to put up with one another's minor or temporary neurotic traits. The main psychotherapy available, in practice, for these minor neuroses is the sympathy of our fellows.

Serious mental ill health is a vast specialized subject. Here it is appropriate only to mention some of the general characteristics of such illness. *Schizophrenia* is characterized by a gradual withdrawal from the world of objective reality. Thinking becomes bizarre, emotions become dead, and the patient lives in a private world, real only for him. It is the pathological form of one of the general human reactions to problems—that of withdrawal and escape. In its *paranoid* form schizophrenia is characterized by highly systematic delusions of being persecuted. This is the pathological state corresponding to the normal phenomenon of 'touchiness.' Pathological *depression* and *anxiety* explain themselves. They are analogous to the ordinary states, but developed to such a nightmarish or serious degree that they require medical treatment. There are also some *organic psychoses*, or mental illnesses associated with a physical cause, such as a brain tumour. Since there are controllable factors which determine partly whether a person will remain on the good or unfortunate side of the mental health scale, there is justification for some policy of encouraging positive mental health, despite the reservation made in the preceding paragraph.

The Underwood report on maladjusted children (1956) recommends, as part of a mental health policy, that (a) there should be a child-guidance clinic for every 45,000 children, (b) the clinics should co-operate with child-welfare centres, (c) health visitors should study mental as well as physical health, (d) there should be short courses on mental health for doctors, (e) there should be more discussion groups and clubs for parents, (f) students preparing to be teachers should study mental health, and (g) simple pamphlets on child care should be prepared for parents. Each child-guidance clinic would be staffed with one psychiatrist, two educational psychologists, and three psychiatric social workers. (The P.S.W.s, as they are called, are responsible for studying and helping the homes of the children.)

In 1954 there were 300 child-guidance clinics, mostly part-time, in England and Wales. Of these, 204 were provided by local education authorities. Clinics can play a valuable rôle in diagnosing and treating backwardness, maladjustment, and delinquency. They are an essential part of an ideal school service, for there are problems which teachers cannot deal with in the classroom. Clinics have sometimes been too few to cope adequately with the children referred to them. Obtaining good staff can also be a problem. When the ideal is reached there remain problems which are too deeply rooted in society to yield even to the special care of a clinic.

More recent psychiatric theory gives less emphasis to the old division into conscious and unconscious. Instead, the single concept of observable behaviour is considered adequate for psychiatric purposes, although such behaviour varies in its susceptibility to analysis by the person manifesting it, or by another person, such as a psychiatrist. Similarly, motives are not discrete psychic forces which mysteriously drive us along, but rather verbal designations of observed patterns of behaviour. This represents an attempt to reconcile the psychological insight of the earlier psychoanalysts with the biological, experimental view

which emphasizes the criterion of observable behaviour.
Modern behaviourism, while retaining much of the flavour
of its earlier forms, gives fuller recognition to symbolic
functioning and to the organism's interpretation of its
environment.

Masserman (1946) gives accounts of experiments in
which animals reacted to conflict and stress in ways which
might previously have been called typically human. Rats
deprived of water ate or hoarded more food than usual,
just as war-time shortages may make human beings hoard
material which is not immediately needed. Cats continued
to press a food-releasing switch even when satisfied, just
as human beings pile up profits even when their needs are
satisfied. Where animals were confronted with conflict-
producing choices they became hypersensitive to all stimuli,
went off their food, withdrew from the problem into
immobility or hyperactivity, surrendered their dominance,
indulged in less sexual activity and less preening, or behaved
with suspiciousness, restlessness, or impulsiveness. These are
common neurotic symptoms. Animals which were given
the free run of their laboratories were less susceptible to
neurosis, just like healthy human beings who are given
adequate scope to explore the world, or mental-hospital
patients who are now given spacious grounds in which to
roam, and who are, if possible, freed from the close
confinement which was once thought indispensable.

Just as Masserman's animals developed neuroses comparable with those of human beings, so they could be cured
by such typical devices as prolonged removal from the
conflict situation, guidance and retraining, and social
contact with healthy animals. While there is, of course, no
elaborate or verbal symbolism in animals as there is in
men, the earliest beginnings of symbolism are present in
the animals' temporary acceptance of symbolic rewards.
Chimpanzees have been taught to accept temporarily the

reward of poker-chips instead of food. Like young children, the chimpanzees had to be able to cash their chips for the real thing without too much delay. Some people have been alarmed by the alleged reduction of human beings to the level of animals. Such alarm is not justified. Human experience is valuable in itself, however it may be analysed. There is reason for criticism only where the tone of the analysts is derogatory and 'clever,' as it sometimes is.

While psychotherapists from Freud onward have provided such interesting insight into human mentality, some of their doctrines and practices have been subjected to still fiercer criticism than any mentioned earlier in this chapter. Eysenck (1953) has argued that many of their assertions are unsupported by evidence of a strictly scientific nature. Psychoanalysts, in particular, are criticized for using unreliable data, for confusing data and interpretation, for generalizing beyond the evidence, and for generally begging questions. Even at the practical level of psychotherapy, he argues, evidence shows that the same proportion of neurotics (two out of three) gets better, whether treatment is psychoanalytic, eclectic, or just the general supervision provided by an ordinary doctor. He rejects the Freudian emphasis on environmental sources of neuroses and claims that proneness to neuroses is a largely heritable property of the nervous system. Evidence is quoted to show that different psychiatrists make different diagnoses of the mental health of the same group of individuals. Their disagreement may be of the magnitude of 31 per cent. of the cases. Stafford-Clark (1952) quotes evidence to suggest that physical treatments of the psychoneuroses (by electricity, insulin, or surgery, for example) can increase the proportion of improvements, can reduce the length of the period of treatment, and can effect improvements in particularly severe cases.

Stafford-Clark also makes a statement which throws

light on the whole business of psychotherapy : "For all the wisdom, skill, and technical accomplishment which ought to go into it, psychotherapy is fundamentally but another way of using the creative power of love towards the restoration of human happiness and peace of mind." This reminds us that mental health in the family, the school, the college, or any other part of the community depends on practical understanding of, and unselfish help for, other people.

Chapter Thirteen

A Biological View of Man

MANY psychologists have endeavoured to assimilate the study of mankind to the general biological sciences, and the purpose of this chapter is to outline some of the main features of this attempt. Some thinkers have felt that the biological approach is unworthy of such a mighty topic as man, tending to represent him as "but a monkey shaved." If this has been true in some writings, it is not necessarily true. The view taken in this book is that psychological truth should be sought between the arrogance which sets man apart from the rest of nature and the lack of subtlety, which considers that the richness of human experience can be exhaustively explained in terms of animal instincts and activities.

The habit of reading human explanations into what are only animal or inanimate phenomena is called 'anthropomorphism.' It means giving human shape to things that are not distinctively human. For example, it is very human to speak about 'the cheerful robin,' but it is less certain that the robin brings as much cheer to himself as he does to us. Anthropomorphism is the very stuff of fable literature, and the literary device of 'personification,' which every schoolboy *ought* to know, is another version of this human tendency. The scientific approach, on the contrary, shuns all reference to human motives and experiences until the operations of instinct and reflex have been fully used. David Lack (1953) describes some of the curious ways in

which robins may behave. Robins would posture threaten-
ingly or actually attack a stuffed robin, even if the stuffed
model was mounted sideways or upside-down. In fact, half
the robins presented with a mere bundle of red and white
breast-feathers on a wire displayed typical threat-posturing.
The robins clearly have a different 'understanding' of such
a situation from that of human beings, and yet some
human behaviour is equally irrational, as when the very
mention of 'Russia' or 'capitalism' or 'intelligence tests' or
'income tax' is a red feather to different groups of 'robins'
whom you can imagine. Also, even robins have a wide
range of individuality of which the scientific observer must
learn to take account. "A few," writes Mr Lack, "ignored
the stuffed bird altogether, some attacked only feebly and
briefly, others for rather longer, and some violently."

The word 'instinct' is often used to refer to patterns of
behaviour that are largely fixed and invariable in all the
members of a given species. Creatures like ants and bees
live their lives according to such patterns, and even the
biological functions of getting food and of reproducing the
species may devolve separately upon different groups
within the species. Here there is little individuality,
variability, or intelligence, by comparison with human
behaviour, although Morley (1953) claims that the mental
powers of ants should not be underrated, and that "they
can learn the correct route in simple mazes which have six
blind-alleys, and individual ants vary in their ability to do
this and in the speed (or number of runs through the maze)
in which they learn their lesson." Whatever their intelligence, ants have existed for millions of years. If the
biological criterion of success is survival, then it is unfortunate that ants are unable to feel proud of themselves.
Since human beings, rightly or wrongly, would hardly
accept ants as being nature's greatest success, we must seek
for another criterion. It is difficult to do so without resort-

ing to considerations that are biological only in an extremely wide sense.

It is usual to consider not only the length of survival of a species (which would put man far in the rear) but also the complexity of what does survive. Man has a stronger claim here, but complexity, of itself, is not a virtue. Another attempt to express man's superiority in purely biological terms is to claim that his adjustment to the environment has outstripped that of other species in virtue of his immense scientific control of the world. But this is a return to a claim based on size and complexity of control. It is not obvious that ants and bees are worse adjusted to their environments, although their adjustment is within a smaller scope. Man, with his larger world, has more maladjustments as well as good adjustments to it. The ant, we presume, does not know what he is missing, and cannot feel any worse off. Man cannot readily base his claim to superiority on simple biological conceptions. We know what it means to be heirs of the glorious and inglorious past, to understand and control the other living creatures on the earth, to adventure and love and speculate and reflect, to perceive wisdom and loveliness, and we would not exchange this for another life in which we have no reason to believe that these things exist.

All the adventures of the spirit, however, must take place within material frameworks. There is the physical environment into which we are born. It may be the extreme heat and wet of a tropical community, the moderate climate of a corner of England, an Arctic community in northern Alaska, a remote Pacific island or Tibetan mountain village, a grim industrial city, a clean and lovely countryside, a shack with few amenities, a luxury apartment, a municipal housing-scheme, a suburban village, a farmhouse, a slum. Each separate environment represents a separate group of possibilities and limitations for those born into it. Moreover, the possibilities and limitations are not only the obvious physical ones, but also the physiological, psychological, medical, and social circumstances that accompany them. Even within one community, especially if it is a large modern community, there are sub-communities in which the physical environments are radically different. Teachers and administrators have to strive towards a sympathetic appreciation of these, even when their own upbringing may have prevented them from realizing just how other groups live. The chance of being born into this or that community inevitably shapes life in particular ways during the very years when children are most impressionable and personalities are being founded.

Secondly, there is the immediate physical environment constituted by our own bodies. We may be destined for fatness or leanness, muscularity or flaccidity, good health or recurrent illness, poor eyesight or exceptional hearing; for beauty or deformity, dexterity or clumsiness, shortness or tallness, whiteness, blackness, or yellowness. Not all these are purely constitutional, and the psychological implications may be extremely varied in relation even to one physical feature. But these physical phenomena do increase the chances of one thing happening, of one choice being made, of one experience being had, rather than others. Apart from the limitations that are set upon particular individuals, there are general limitations that affect almost all. Most of us cannot count on living to be 100, or even 90 or 80. Most of us cannot—even if we wanted to— aspire to the four-minute mile. We are, like all species, given only a certain range of accomplishments.

Thirdly, we live in a world of catastrophes, although most of us are sensible enough to forget about the fact for most of the time. Past and less scientific ages were more impressed by physical catastrophes, for they had fewer means of controlling them. But still to-day fire, flood, storm, and tempest destroy life, however heavily insured. Even the wealthiest communities have their own catastrophes, and thrombosis strikes down the business executive more often than the worker in the fields.

The fourth limiting factor has been left to the end. It is not the least important nor the least controversial. Our physical inheritance is the first in time to determine the possibilities of our lives. We do not know a great deal about human inheritance, but we know more than formerly. The nucleus of a body-cell contains chromosomes, so called because they take a deep stain. Chromosomes are understood to consist, in turn, of strings of genes which cannot be seen, but which are inferred to be the ultimate determiners of inherited qualities. Human body-cells contain twenty-three pairs of chromosomes. The male has one pair referred to as X and Y, the female a pair both referred to as X. When mating takes place the fused spermatozoon and ovum does not, as one might suppose, have forty-six pairs of chromosomes. It takes only half from each parent cell, so that the newly-started organism will have twenty-three pairs of chromosomes, just like its parents. The sex of the new organism is determined by what happens to the X's and Y's. It is father who, in a sense, determines the matter. Mother has nothing but X's to give. Father can contribute his X, in which case the baby will be a girl; or he can contribute Y, in which case the baby will be an XY, another male. Sex and all the differences that result from being a man or a woman thus have their origin in the chance result of this genetical algebra. The X and Y chromosomes influence characteristics other than sex. These are said to be sex-linked.

Gregor Mendel was an Austrian monk and abbot of the Moravian monastery of Brünn. In 1865 he published a paper in the Journal of the Brünn Society of Natural History. It was only in 1900 that this paper was unearthed by the Amsterdam professor De Vries, and its importance recognized. Mendel carried out breeding experiments with plants in his monastery garden and argued that the results could be explained in a certain way. New varieties of plant did not, in this view, develop gradually. Rather there were sudden changes in the genetical constitution of the plant seed, giving rise to new varieties.

Charles Darwin (1809-82) and Gregor Mendel (1822-84) did not come across one another's work, but we can understand how they complement one another. If we consider the varieties of plant that spring up quite suddenly from genetical changes, how do some varieties survive and others not? Here Darwin's principle of natural selection provides the answer. Those varieties that are favoured by their environment survive; those that are not, perish. Modern biologists have advanced beyond the simplicity of this view, but still accept its essential truth.

The doctrine of Lamarck (1744-1829) that new varieties and functions develop through use—that, for example, parents who live a life of muscular toil will enable their children to inherit better muscles—is exploded. Neo-Lamarckians have argued ingeniously on behalf of the inheritance of acquired characteristics, but their most plausible examples can normally be better explained in terms of the Darwinian hypothesis. If muscular parents have muscular children it is not because of the parents' acquired capacity but because they transmit the genetical basis of good muscles. There is only one way in which qualities are inherited and that is via the genes. It would be misleading to say this without indicating that a great deal has yet to be learned about how the genes determine particular traits in humans.

In Mendelian theory certain traits are thought of as recessive and others as dominant. When Mendel crossed tall and dwarf pea-plants the resulting hybrids were all tall. He considered tallness, therefore, a dominant character in this particular plant. He proceeded to cross the hybrid tall plants to see what happened : three-quarters were tall, one-quarter dwarf. He took his experiment a generation further by crossing the plants of the second generation : some crossings resulted in tall plants only and some in dwarf plants only, but some produced both tall and dwarf. The striking thing is that, where both kinds were produced, the ratio was preserved of three-quarters tall and one-quarter dwarf. In brief, there was a mathematical regularity in the products of hybrid breeding. Here was the start of the science of genetics.

In man genes are not such that one gene determines one inherited characteristic. Several genes may influence a single observable characteristic. This is so of eye, hair, and skin colour in man. Crossing diverse sets of chromosomes may bring disharmonizing genes together, so that, for example, a man has a large body and a small heart, long legs and short arms, or something similar. In addition, genes change their nature spontaneously—these changes are called mutations—and give rise to new characteristics. These are often disadvantageous and are weeded out by the process of natural selection, or perhaps one should say, natural rejection. One direct outside influence that increases the rate of mutations is that of X-rays.

Despite our increased knowledge of genetics, the old problem of the relative importance of heredity and environment remains intransigently with us. Those who face it are not always free from prejudice. The advocates of change like to believe that environments can be altered and human nature with them. The more conservative emphasize the limitations imposed by heredity. Hollingshead (1942) found that the top class in one American community emphasized the importance of inheriting "good blood." (Strictly speaking, they should have said "good

genes," for blood is not the carrier of inherited characters.)
The second top class, half of whom had made their way
upward by education, was much more inclined to stress
the importance of education for success in life. The third
and middle social class had the interestingly inconsistent
attitude that their own failure to rise further sprang from
the upper classes' keeping them down, whereas the failure
of the lower classes to rise to the middle was due to their
bad heredity. The fourth class was contented to consider
itself "the backbone of the community," while the fifth
was "passive and fatalistic."

At one time people tried to demonstrate the influence of
heredity by tracing family-trees. Many long genealogies
were traced, either of genius and artistic talent, or of crime,
low intelligence, and vice. These are interesting but do not
prove much, for the brilliant genealogies are often matched
by highly favourable circumstances, just as the deplorable
genealogies are often of people whose environment was
poverty-stricken and squalid.

The most critical test of the contributions made by
heredity and environment would be the comparison of
identical twins, born after the splitting of a single ovum
and subsequently reared apart; or of non-identical twins,
born after the fertilization of two separate ova at the same
time, and subsequently reared together. The identical twins
come from the same egg, and therefore have precisely the
same inherited pattern of chromosomes and genes. Any
differences produced in them after they have been
separated for some time must be due to the differing
environments. The non-identical twins come from the
fusion of two quite different pairs of spermatozoa and ova.
Their chromosomes and genes are no more alike than those
of brothers and sisters born of the same parents. It just
happens that the separate fertilized ova develop in the
mother at the same time. If these non-identical twins are

raised in the same environment after birth (as they inevitably are before birth), then any differences in their characters must be due to inheritance. These requirements are easier to state than to obtain in practice. The available evidence is neither copious nor very cogent.

In the 1947 Scottish mental survey 468 pairs of twins aged 11 years were tested. Their average I.Q. was about 5 points lower than the average of non-twins. The I.Q.s of pairs of like-sex twins correlated to the extent of +0.73, and of unlike-sex twins to the extent of +0.63, compared with the usual correlation of +0.5 between siblings who are not twins. Cole (1939), who stresses environmental influences at the expense of genetical, comments on earlier examples of such correlations :

> Why should the fraternal twins show any greater resemblance than siblings, if the genes are solely responsible? Does it not indicate that being born at the same period in the family history and meeting the same events at the same period (and ages) has a greater chance of inducing identity? And is it not equally possible that the identity in sex and appearance may call for an identity of treatment, of reaction from the social environment, in the case of the identicals, which is not produced in the other cases?

Valentine (1956) urges the common-sense argument that children brought up in very similar environments develop very different talents and personalities. He writes :

> A large number of children from the poorest and worst types of homes do far better in intelligence tests than do many children from the homes of higher social or economic or cultural levels; and even in half a dozen children of the same family the range of intelligence may be enormous.

Eysenck (1952) describes a study of sixty-eight pairs of identical twins. To ensure as far as possible that they really were identical twins, a great number of physical tests were used. Then the twins did seventeen other tests designed to assess what Eysenck calls "the neurotic dimension." On these seventeen personality assessments the group of identical twins correlated to the extent of $+0.851$.

Newman, Freeman, and Holzinger (1937) studied fifty pairs of identical twins, fifty pairs of fraternal twins of like sex (all reared in pairs), and nineteen pairs of identical twins who had been separated. They found that, on the whole, physical traits and general ability tended most to be dependent upon heredity, and achievement, personality, and temperament to be less so. Even where correlational and other studies may suggest a strong hereditary influence, we are far from being able to analyse the nature of this in terms of chromosomes and genes. We must distinguish (a) qualities, such as intelligence, that appear to be largely inherited; (b) conditions which may exist at birth (congenital) without being inherited—e.g., infantile syphilis; and (c) conditions of which the precise genetic determination is known—e.g., hæmophilia, which is genetically transmitted by the female but manifests itself in males.

As far as applied psychology is concerned, environmental variation is most important. Even if eugenic dictators attempted to improve the genetic quality of a community by controlling matings there is little biological evidence (quite apart from moral considerations) to suggest that their endeavours would be successful. Teachers and parents must therefore seek salvation in environmental controls, and accept what is inherited as it stands.

We are not concerned here with blood circulation, respiration, digestion, reproduction, or the special senses, as such. But the central nervous system, the autonomic nervous system, and the endocrine glands have a very direct bearing upon our psychological lives. Some writers have made our mental life seem only a by-product of these systems. Such a view is not taken here, but something will be said about each of the three. There is no intention of giving even a full popular account of these, but only of recalling their vital part in the pattern of man's experience.

The central nervous system consists essentially of the brain and spinal cord together with the great number of nerve fibres running in and out of these, to and from all the parts of the body. It is via the central nervous system that we see, hear, feel, smell, and taste, the world in which we live. And it is via this system that the parts of our body are moved to do our will or to carry out those reflex actions which are part of our make-up. A great deal is now known about the relationship between various kinds of behaviour and experience and various specific parts of the central nervous system. We know which parts of the cerebral cortex (surface of the brain) are specialized to deal with nerve impulses coming along nerve fibres from the various special sensory organs. Visual stimulation, for example, sends impulses along the optic nerve to the occipital lobe at the back of the brain. To speak about such things is to over-simplify them, for in reality they are extremely complex. The retina of the human eye alone has one hundred million end-organs.

Nerve impulses are not different in kind for the different senses. A nerve impulse is a nerve impulse wherever it happens. What really distinguishes between visual and auditory experience, physiologically speaking, is their different geographical origins and termini. Visual impulses travel between eye and occipital lobe, auditory between ear and temporal lobe. The size of the area of the cortex devoted to any one sense is related to the importance of that sense to the species concerned. Vision is an important human sense and is represented by a large area of the cortex. In a Shetland pony, Adrian relates, the cortical area for smell is as large as all the rest together, while in the pig the area for smell is the exclusive sensory receiving-area. There are also differences in the sizes of the areas

dealing with impulses to and from the various general parts
of the human body. The face, with its expressiveness and
sensitivity, has a bigger share of the areas receiving tactile
impulses from, and sending motor impulses to, the muscles
than a part of the body which we use less for sensing or
handling the outside world.

Man is the species in which the frontal lobes of the
brain are most developed (perhaps a justification of the
term 'highbrow'), and yet they can be removed without loss
of memory for particular events or skills. Similarly,
memories can survive widespread destruction of the right
half of the brain. The study of the effects of losing part of
the brain through accident or operative necessity has contributed to our understanding of the functions served by
different parts of the brain.

Another modern approach to brain functions is that of
electro-encephalography, or the recording of electrical
impulses produced by the brain itself. Three typical electrical rhythms are found. The *alpha* rhythm of about 10
impulses per second is found at the back of the brain, a
beta rhythm of about 20 impulses per second at the front,
and possibly a *theta* rhythm of about 6 impulses per second
in the middle. During sleep a *delta* rhythm of 0.5 to 3.5
impulses per second appears. The *alpha* rhythm increases
during repose and the *beta* during excitement. The
rhythms of identical twins are almost as similar as their
fingerprints. The rhythms are not correlated with intelligence test results. Walter (1953), an enthusiastic electro-
encephalographer, writes :

> Intelligence, as estimated by arbitrary and already obsol-
> escent tests, finds no parallel in our tracings; but versatility,
> ductility, and certain special imaginative aptitudes are
> beginning to be recognized as dynamic interrelations and
> transformations within the framework of normal variation.

This overestimates our understanding of 'brain-waves' and underestimates the evidence about intelligence tests.

The autonomic nervous system also has a wide dominion throughout our bodies. The nerves of this system go to the heart muscle, the involuntary muscles of all blood-vessels and of the stomach and intestines, to the sweat glands, the pupils of the eyes, the salivary glands, and the larynx. This system maintains the tone of all muscles and regulates those bodily happenings which are involuntary. It is through this system that our strong emotions of fear or excitement find bodily expression, Indeed, it has been maintained that the autonomic excitement comes first in response to some outside stimulus, and that our emotions are a by-product of the autonomic events. According to this, the James-Lange theory of emotion, we are frightened because we sweat and tremble, and not the other way round. Such a simple paradox has not, however, been borne out by experiment. Cole, reviewing the history of this question, endorses the view of the physiologist W. B. Cannon. According to this, the *consciousness* of emotion is associated with the cortex, but it is the thalamus (in the middle of the brain) which correlates the patterns of emotional *expression*. Thus an ordinary sensation reaching the cortex via the thalamus would have an emotional colouring. Like so many human matters, this one is marked by complexity which is not easy to unravel. Whatever the detailed operation of emotional experiences and reactions, it is the autonomic nervous system which makes us palpitate or sweat or tremble or flush or swallow or have queer feelings in our stomachs with the excitement of anger or fear or delight.

The third bodily system that has a direct bearing on our psychological states is that of the endocrine or ductless glands, already mentioned in our discussion of "Personality." These glands send their secretions directly into the

blood-stream in amounts which are small but of great
significance. The main ductless glands are the pituitary,
thyroid, adrenal, and sex glands. The pituitary is complex
and secretes at least eight different hormones (from the
Greek *horman*, to stir up). These pituitary hormones
control growth, stimulate certain muscles, and regulate
sexual functioning. The adrenal hormones are *cortin*, which
affects the growth and development of the sex glands, and
adrenalin, which has widespread effects in preparing the
body for an emergency. Typical adrenalin effects are
dilation of the pupil of the eye, increased heartbeat, relaxed
bronchi, inhibited digestion, conversion of glycogen from
the liver into glucose, and widespread changes in the blood
circulation. *Thyroxin* from the thyroid gland is necessary
in tiny amounts (as little as 12 mg. active in the body at a
given time). Deficiency can cause a person to be apathetic
and dull-witted, and a child may become the kind of
mental defective known as a 'cretin.' An excess can make
a person over-active, anxious, and emotional. These conditions of glandular deficiency or excess are, of course,
exceptional, and are far from being the most common
causes of dull wits or over-activity. The sex glands, or
gonads, are concerned with reproduction and with all the
physical characteristics that distinguish men and women.
In women, sex hormones also regulate the menstrual cycle
and pregnancy.

Behaviourism is the name of the psychological outlook
which attempts to explain everything in terms of the
environment working on the body, without recourse to
'mentalistic' terms. J. B. Watson, a famous name in the
earlier history of behaviourism, was prepared (in principle!) to take any baby of sound body and make him
into a doctor or a tramp. Mental phenomena were just the
offshoots of behaviour. Modern behaviourists are less
extreme, but still concentrate on exhausting physiological

explanations before resorting to the 'mental,' 'spiritual,' or 'psychic.' They sometimes trail their coats, attacking animism or anthropomorphism with as much zest as Don Quixote attacked the windmill.

Julian Huxley (1941) suggests five aspects of man's uniqueness :

(1) The capacity for conceptual thought and the maintenance of traditions.

(2) Greater variability in reproducing and in the environments which he can tolerate.

(3) The absence of mutually infertile groups, and consequently of biological divergence.

(4) The absence of a special breeding season.

(5) The length and relative importance of the developmental period after physical maturity has been reached.

The first would seem to be greatest in importance to man himself, even if the others have been necessary. In whatever detail our physical and physiological limitations are unfolded, it is the living of their lives that matters to people. If the physiological correlates of every subtlest human experience were defined, only physiologists would attend to them. And even they, outside their laboratories, would live for the pleasure and adventure of living.

Chapter Fourteen

A Social View of Man

WHILE the physiologists emphasize the bodily framework of human experience, the social psychologists and sociologists stress those human characteristics that result from belonging to groups, whether informal or formal. The social psychologist is interested in how individual psychology is modified by the influences of group membership. The sociologist has similar interests but is more concerned with the formal structure of society and with wide social and economic influences. Both kinds of problem affect the work of teachers and the education of children. Examples of the first kind are: What groups do children form when left to themselves? What kinds of children emerge as leaders in such groups? What makes a child popular with a group of his fellows? What are the influences of gang-life upon boys at certain ages? How can teachers use group psychology for educational purposes? Examples of the second kind are: What educational limitations or influences are inherent in the societies from which children come? How far can teachers enlist such influences in furthering school work, and how far are they obliged to accept its circumscription by more potent forces?

McDougall's *Introduction to Social Psychology*, first published in 1908, was a dominant influence in this sphere of study during the first half of the twentieth century. McDougall traced the most highly developed qualities of human experience to a limited number of fundamental *instincts*. He defined an instinct as an inherited or innate psychophysical disposition which determines its possessor to perceive, and to pay attention to, objects of a certain class, to experience an emotional excitement of a particular quality upon perceiving such an object, and to act in regard to it in a particular manner, or, at least, to experience an impulse to such action.

Some of the main instincts, together with their corresponding emotions, were those of flight (fear), repulsion (disgust), exploration (curiosity), pugnacity (anger), self-abasement (submission), self-assertion (elation), parental care (tenderness), reproduction (sexual excitement), acquisitiveness (joy of possession), and construction (joy of creation). In each case McDougall tried to show that the particular instinct was universal and that it manifested itself in distinctive qualities of observation, emotion, and striving. The awakening of the reproductive instinct in adolescents would cause them to pay more attention to members of the opposite sex, to feel sexually excited as part of a sentiment of love, and to strive to win the favour of those they love. The complexity of instinctive patterns in man was fully recognized. Both the stimuli bringing an instinct into operation and the responses which followed were extremely variable in man, compared with the narrower ranges of stimulus and response in animals. In addition, the basic instincts in human beings combined into complex *sentiments*. A blend of submission, fear, wonder, and tenderness would, for example, give rise to the sentiment of reverence.

Psychologists of the behaviourist school have criticized instinct theory, particularly on the grounds that it is not sufficiently based on precise physiological knowledge. Human behaviour may be classified into any number of 'psychophysical dispositions' according to personal taste, but this does not explain in concrete terms what a psychophysical disposition is. McDougall's retort to this criticism was that he welcomed every expansion of our physiological understanding, but no physiological knowledge would alter the facts (*a*) that it is in man's nature to strive towards certain goals, and (*b*) that the process of becoming aware of these goals and of taking appropriate action to achieve them is a cognitive activity—an activity of knowing, however vague. He called his psychology 'hormic,' meaning that it explains human behaviour in terms of striving towards goals.

Even if a long list of specific goals is unsatisfactory it is still useful to describe the general goals towards which men strive. And if these general kinds provide an unsatisfactory psychological analysis it is still of the essence of science to try to reduce the multiplicity of phenomena to the simplicity of a few categories.

Nunn (1920) gave educational expression to McDougall's hormic outlook.

> In every act we say to our world, openly or implicitly, "I am here and to be reckoned with; I go a way that is, so far as may be, my own way and not merely yours." And our bodies say the same thing after their own manner. Throughout the whole range of life this attitude prevails, from the amœba, in which it is but a bare, unconscious 'will to live,' to man, who consciously claims a share in the moulding of his own destiny.

McDougall listed gregariousness as one of his instincts, although it had no specific emotion associated with it. It was based on a 'consciousness of kind' and tended to bring people together even where there was no particular justification. They congregated in cities even where they *could* have led a pastoral life (he instances Australia). Once there, they congregated in sub-groups according to similarity of tastes. A modern social psychologist would put forward subtler considerations about man's 'gregariousness.' Harding (1953), for example, speaks of "three broad features of [man's] social life, individual activities carried out with social sanction, interests shared with those around him, and a place within a network of social companionship." One may feel home-sick among a crowd of people.

Stagner and Karwoski (1952) accept Klineberg's classification of motives into (a) those that are physiological and absolutely predictable (e.g., hunger); (b) those that have a physiological basis but are not universally predictable (e.g., sex); (c) those that have general physiological concomitants in the autonomic nervous system and in the endocrine system, but which are less predictable (e.g., fear, anger); and (d) those that occur relatively frequently but have no specific physiological basis (e.g., the social motives, such as the desire for esteem). This view recognizes both the physiological basis of much human motivation and the strength of motives which are essentially social. Physiological needs constitute the basis because (a) they come first in the individual's lifetime; (b) in extreme circumstances they are the last to survive; (c) they do not, like cultural needs, vary from country to country; and (d) animal behaviour shows that physiological needs come first on the evolutionary scale of time. Social motives, although they may be derived ultimately from physiological ones, develop a power of their own which may even overcome physiological needs. Instances of human martyrdom are an extreme example. Allport (1938) has called this phenomenon 'functional autonomy.' Some behaviour, originating as a means of satisfying an end, becomes an end in itself. Many things that children do in the first instance to satisfy the curious whims of their parents they later do for their own satisfaction. Even chimpanzees have a limited power to be satisfied with symbolic rewards rather than substantial rewards such as food.

Social motivation is complex, not simple. Its higher forms require abstention from the present satisfaction of simple needs in order to achieve the future satisfaction of a

complex need—for example, the need to succeed in a skilled
job. When something goes wrong with a complex satisfaction those participating in the situation may regress to
much simpler satisfactions by way of compensation.
Unhappy adults may spend their afternoons in the teashop
or their evenings in the bar.

At the beginning of the century the American philos-
opher and educationist John Dewey experimented with,
and wrote about, a new educational method. Part of his
belief was that the virtues of being educated together, and
of children educating one another by co-operative effort,
should be exploited. This has been called 'socializing education.' Society is thought to be educative in so far as people
share purposes and interests. "The very process of living
together educates." If educators will give more recognition
to this in their practice, then "the native powers of the
young" will have a freer chance to operate, "initiative in
coping with novel situations" will be increased, and
personal perception will be valued above drill. Dewey
admits that "the quality and value of the socialization
depends upon the habits and aims of the group," but "a
democratic society repudiates the principle of external
authority." Whatever aims are adopted must be consistent
with economic equality (presumably of opportunity) and
with free social interchange. Here is an educational policy
that lays strong emphasis on social psychology. Does such
a policy work in practice?

For several decades educators, according to their varying
lights, have tried, especially in the United States and
Canada, to have their children learn by co-operating in
'projects.' There is general agreement that for young
children, and under skilled management, this co-operative
learning can combine academic progress with a richness
of associated experience and an abundant zest in the
process of learning which were untypical of scholastic

learning in previous centuries. The observation of children at play, or of the added enjoyment which adults often obtain from sharing activities with others, reveals something of the power of social motives. It can be readily agreed, too, that there is much value in learning to co-operate with other people. But beyond this point 'socialized' learning becomes a less certain advantage. Older children can profit from co-operative methods, but as their individual talents become increasingly specialized, and as the more intelligent outstrip the less intelligent, it becomes increasingly necessary to abandon universal co-operation. The co-operative groups have to be more selectively composed. Individuals must not be tied within the limitations of the group. Original work springs ultimately from individual effort. Even with younger children the zest of competition is relished as keenly as the joys of co-operation, and need not be discouraged so long as it is incidental and not all-absorbing. Co-operation can become as much of a tyrant as competition. Children may be taught to seem co-operative and social-minded when they feel very differently. The foisting of 'socialization' in half-baked and imperceptive forms upon the schools has brought its own counter-attack from outraged parents and educators. Dewey to some extent caricatured traditional educational aims and methods. He himself has now been travestied in practice and in report. Such is the swing of the historical pendulum.

Leadership is a quality that is often stressed by educators and that social psychologists have attempted to analyse. Wall (1955) writes:

Usually leadership comes to those who possess, in the eyes of the group, in a concentrated and well-defined form, certain apparent qualities which themselves correspond to the group's values, aspirations, and fears, both consciously held and unconsciously determined.

Social psychologists have studied groups to find which
persons do take the lead in action and which persons are
preferred as leaders, as indicated by the choices of other
members of the group. In war-time it is important to find
good leaders at many levels, and in the Second World War
the problem of leadership received much attention. Harris
(1949) gives a detailed and interesting account of procedures used to select officers. For the present purpose, a
summary of fifteen factors that he considers relevant to
military leadership is sufficient to show how leadership is a
complex quality and not a simple one. The criteria he
suggests are :

    (1) A record of past social participation and responsibility.
    (2) A report on recent efficiency, interests, character, etc.
    (3) An intelligence rating commensurate with the kind of
        leadership under consideration.
    (4) An educational standard commensurate with the kind
        of leadership under consideration.
    (5) An appropriate level of aspiration or ambition.
    (6) A degree of practical effectiveness commensurate with
        the level of aspiration.
    (7) A thorough identification of oneself with the field of
        leadership in question.
    (8) Planning ability.
    (9) Width of interests.
  (10) Warm spontaneity in behaviour.
  (11) Objectivity of outlook.
  (12) Capacity for firmness.
  (13) Tact.
  (14) Ability to bring others into the picture.
  (15) Personal stability.[1]

These factors are not independent. They overlap—or in
other words, they are positively correlated—to some

[1] Adapted from *The Group Approach to Leadership Testing* (Routledge
and Kegan Paul, 1949), pp. 225-226.

extent. They are, however, useful pointers to the complex quality of leadership.

Gregor Ziemer (1942), who was President of the American Colony School in Berlin, described the system of Nazi educational leadership and propaganda. This is a study in leading people into evil. The young were educated to obey the Fuehrer unquestioningly, to accept death, to worship the State and nation, and to hate the Jews and foreigners. The whole educational system was controlled by detailed decree. Aggression, endurance, and militarism were encouraged, with a universal emphasis on physical education. Strong emotions were inculcated with reference to such words as 'blood' and 'soil.' The nationalist ideal of an expanding, conquering state was upheld. *Elements* of such an outlook are to be found in many communities, from large states to small schools. They represent a degree of mental ill-health from which the rest of the community is normally saved by its own good sense, but which may spread rapidly in times of crisis or of thoughtlessness.

Moreno (1953) has discussed at length the nature of social structures and the ineluctably social character of human life. He describes various techniques of measuring social structures and of improving them. *Sociometric testing* consists in finding out the social preferences of a group of people in relation to a specific criterion. Suppose that a teacher has to allocate a class of children to several huts in a holiday camp. If he were solving the problem sociometrically he would begin by warming the children to an interest in the problem, so that they would answer questions sincerely. Then he would ask each child to write down the companions he would prefer to have and those he would prefer not to have. The details can be varied, but eventually there emerges a pattern of choices and rejections which should, in Moreno's view, enable the best allocation to be made. The method assumes that there is a strong, enduring, and definite criterion that will evoke sincere and spontaneous choices and rejections by the members of the group.

The pattern of choices and rejections can be represented pictorially in a *sociogram*. It is claimed that the geometrical

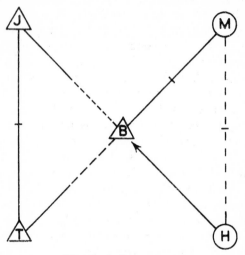

Fig. 8. A SOCIOGRAM

John and Ted choose one another. John and Ted also choose Bill. Bill rejects Ted and is indifferent to John. Bill and Mary choose one another. Mary and Helen reject one another. Helen's choice of Bill is not reciprocated in any expressed way.

picture of social choices will reveal social facts that are not obvious to casual observation. A child may be isolated, neither choosing nor being chosen by any other member of a class. Another may be the centre of many choices. Pairs, chains, triangles, stars, and circles of attraction and repulsion will emerge, giving the teacher a better idea of the psychosocial network of a class, always assuming that the members of the group are motivated to be sincere and that the sociometric structure is regularly reviewed in order to detect changes. One of the generalizations suggested by Moreno's work is that the most chosen and least chosen individuals tend to become still more widely differentiated if the group is given further choices. If the total of first choice puts John at the top and Bert at the foot, the addition of the group's second choices to the comparison will reinforce the disparity rather than diminish it.

The idea of spontaneity plays an important part in Moreno's thinking. It refers to the adequacy of a person's response in a new situation or the novelty of his response in a familiar situation. It is the catalysing factor in any live situation. It is experimentally assessed in any person by urging him to throw himself into a state of anger, fear, sympathy, or domination, towards another member of his group, and to act out this emotional relationship. Where Freud practised psychoanalysis and psychotherapy by the method of free verbal association, Moreno advocates a psychodramatic method as being more complete, more alive, more relevant to the present, and more related to the two-way social relationship between people. Related to education, this principle emphasizes plasticity before rigid training, and under-learning as a preparation for spontaneity rather than over-learning as a preparation for repetitive accuracy.

Moreno's discussion of spontaneity is stimulating and suggestive. So are the many techniques and hypotheses that he puts forward, all stressing the hidden as well as the manifest social rôles and networks into which individuals enter. His experiments in combining controlled psychological investigation with the study of complex living situations may seem particularly encouraging to educators. On the debit side, the labour involved in sociometry, the difficulty of obtaining the conditions which are considered essential, and the systematic exclusion or subordination of other than sociometric aims, may limit the applications.

In practice a teacher in the classroom, a headmaster in the school, or anyone who keeps his eyes open in a small community, will see how various cliques are established, how individuals vary in popularity among themselves and from one situation to the next, and how certain individuals are relatively isolated from the surrounding society. The teacher should use such social hierarchies or patterns for his educational purposes where possible, and try to alter the pattern where it seems harmful. This can be done by enlisting the sympathies of existing groups in fresh purposes, or by presenting new causes and values which may lead to the growth of new groups.

While direct verbal persuasion may be partly effective, personal sympathy between teacher and class is still more important in achieving such changes. But both of these may prove insufficient to alter some undesirable social situation. It may take a war to alter society radically, or a family catastrophe to change the family situation. So it may take more dramatic measures to improve a classroom situation. Without subscribing to the doctrine of punishment by 'natural' consequences in its naïvest form, we may find it occasionally necessary to resort to deprivation of privileges, detentions, transfers, expulsions, reports, etc., to bring home to a child or a class that certain behaviour (a) is not in his (or its) own best interests, or (b) is contrary to general values which the teacher knows to be supported by the best human experience.

Modern educational thought has recognized the value of bringing sociological considerations into the classroom and of extending educational considerations outside the classroom. Even when the class teacher can do nothing positive about such considerations a knowledge of them will influence his assessments of children and of their educational needs. Such knowledge may help him to that added measure of understanding and tolerance which underlie humane education. Some teachers misconstrue this to mean that children in unfortunate circumstances should be excused all the time. Such a policy could be almost as inhumane as one of harsh suppression. To temper the wind to the shorn lamb is different from withdrawing an ordinary supply of fresh air.

The *Social Implications of the 1947 Scottish Mental Survey* (1953) provides a good example of the considerations referred to above. This carefully planned and executed study provides an impressive substantiation of the view that

> there is, at one end of the socio-economic scale, the pattern of small families, older parents, more favourable housing conditions, with children above average in intelligence and physique, and at the other end of the scale the large families, low housing standards, poor school-attendance, and children below average in intelligence and in physical development.

It is sometimes argued that social research proves only what everyone knows already. This is not necessarily true. The above inquiry presents quantitative details, not only generalizations. It indicates the need to interpret more critically the popular belief that large families tend to be associated with favourable development. It undermines the once popular belief that high intelligence and good physique tend to be mutually exclusive, and confirms that they are positively correlated. It shows not only that there is a small definite association between family size and height, weight, and intelligence, but that the association persists even inside each occupational class and inside each housing standard.

Apart from carefully limited sociological studies like the

Scottish one just mentioned, there has been a series of large-scale studies of whole communities. Anthropologists have analysed the entire ways of life of old communities relatively uninfluenced by the modern Western world, and sociologists have attempted to deal with modern Western communities in analogous ways. Their work has given rise to the 'culture pattern' school of psychology. Emphasis is laid upon the shaping of individuals by the prevailing outlooks, traditions, educational methods, and general ways of living of the community into which they are born. A culture pattern would develop its own functional autonomy more easily in isolated and conservative communities. Advances in science and in the means of communication disrupt established patterns.

Educators cannot afford to ignore sociology, for sociologists are prone to invade the field of education. Margaret Mead (1944) envisaged social science as helping Americans to follow the pragmatic philosophy which is considered typical of them. Warner and his colleagues (1946) advocated an educational policy derived from sociological considerations. It was argued that the opportunities for economic betterment (or upward mobility) were decreasing in American society, and that, in consequence, it was desirable to devise educational measures which would avoid the over-production of professional workers. The measures included a common curriculum for all during the first six or eight years' schooling, a common curriculum to the extent of one-third of secondary-school studies (the so-called common core), the attachment of more prestige to vocational training in high school, and the encouragement of a 'prestige pyramid' in extra-curricular studies as a consolation for those who were less successful academically. The pros and cons of these views can be debated, but they do illustrate the application of sociological interpretations in educational theory.

The English report on *Early Leaving* (1954) presented evidence that academic progress in secondary schools was strongly associated with the occupational class of fathers. The children of professional and managerial fathers tended to stay at school longer and succeed more than those whose fathers were in other occupational classes. This trend held good whatever the level of success attained by the children before entering the secondary schools. The report recommended more financial aid for able children staying on at school beyond 15. The causes underlying the report's findings are not completely established, but the importance of congenial home surroundings for study and of parental sympathy with the children's education is strongly suggested.

The social influences which perhaps receive most attention are those of the radio, television, films, newspapers, comics, and advertisements. These certainly help to shape the ideas and aspirations of modern communities, and often do so in the direction of what is trivial or materialistic or sordid. They may seem to herald the destruction of the modern generation. On the other hand, what is an unpalatable change for the elders of a community is just the world as they find it for the young, who have known no other. Often the media of communication are condemned (perhaps because of their ever-widening range) when they are only giving a new shape to old virtues and vices. They spread good as well as evil farther afield. Assumptions about the association between films and delinquency, or television and scholastic retardation, have often had to be altered when close investigations have been made. And just as those who are early exposed to a mild degree of infection may be later immune to a virulent attack, so the mass media create a measure of immunity to their own influences. Facilities for travel and sport and social comradeship have also expanded, and, at least with adolescents and young adults, win many victories over other leisure pursuits which are condemned for encouraging passivity.

To regard men as 'the creatures of society' is to underestimate the unique creative quality of individual people, but social psychology and sociology, wisely interpreted, can make a worth-while contribution to human education.

Chapter Fifteen

The Psychologist and the Educator

ALTHOUGH the interests of psychologists and educators overlap to a marked degree, mutual understanding and sympathy have not always been achieved. The aim of this chapter is to sum up the general outlook expressed in the preceding chapters, and to indicate some of the more obvious relationships between psychology and education. Psychologists, as such, are primarily concerned with theorizing about human behaviour and experience, although this in no way implies that they need be impractical or unconcerned about possible applications of theory. Some individual psychologists, including most educational psychologists, devote themselves mainly to applied psychology. Educators, as such, are mainly concerned with changing human behaviour. The changes cannot but be made in accordance with some explicit or implicit philosophy of life. Psychological ideas are only one part of such a philosophy. Physical, moral, æsthetic, and religious notions may bulk larger, despite the fact that many twentieth-century educators have drawn heavily on psychological thinking.

Some ideas and practices that are sanctioned by psychological inquiry have their origins in times which did not know psychology as a distinct subject of scientific study. Psychology owes parts of its own power to circumstances outside itself, such as the advance of analytic and experimental methods, the humanistic emphasis on this life rather than upon any life to come, the need created by democracy to cater for the education of the whole community, and the development of social welfare to include psychological as well as physical benefits.

Modern psychological ideas are most strikingly foreshadowed in Rousseau's *Emile*. He mentions the importance of the early maternal care of a child : "There is no substitute for a mother's love." He refers to the moral influence of the home : "The charms of home are the best antidote to vice." He warns against over-mothering : "The mother may lavish excessive care on her child instead of neglecting him." He knows the influence of mental conflict : "It is mental suffering that leads to despair." He appreciates the importance of the teacher's own education : "How can a child be well educated by one who has not been well educated himself?" He notes the scope and limitations of individual development : "Each progresses more or less according to his genius, his taste, his needs, his talents, his zeal, and his opportunities for using them." He enunciates the principle of giving the child what he needs at each stage of development : "Your child must not get what he asks, but what he needs."

He remarks upon the power of incidental learning : "The lessons the scholars learn from one another in the playground are worth a hundredfold more than what they learn in the classroom." He draws attention to what would now be called the child's ego-involvement : "You must understand that it is no question of applying force, but of arousing some appetite which leads to action, and such an appetite, carefully selected on the lines laid down by nature, kills two birds with one stone." He understands the guiding rôle of the teacher : "The teacher's art consists in this : to turn the child's attention from trivial details and to guide his thoughts continually towards relations of importance which he will one day need to know, that he may judge rightly of good and evil in human society." He sees the need for the careful study of children : "I wish some trust-worthy person would give us a treatise on the art of child-study." His definition of intelligence as the "greater or lesser aptitude for the comparison of ideas and the discovery of relations between them" has some modern support. He finds more danger in ignorance than in knowledge : "It is much less dangerous to satisfy a child's curiosity than to stimulate it."

Rousseau did not, of course, have in his mind the full modern connotation of these ideas. But from the stand-point of practical wisdom Rousseau's statements are perhaps as lucid and cogent as any that have been made more recently. The psychology, like the philosophy, of education is deep-rooted in the past, and has not sprung full-blown from the modern laboratory, as one is some-times invited to imagine. Even before Rousseau, Locke, at the end of the seventeenth century, had argued for the superiority of a positive discipline of esteem over a nega-tive discipline of chastisement; for carrying "everyone's natural genius . . . as far as it could"; for heedfully laying hold of "the favourable Seasons of Aptitude and Inclina-tion"; and for studying Latin by the direct method, and without lengthy memorizations. It would not be true to say that there is nothing new under the sun, but many a modern guise conceals an ancient body underneath. It might be allowed that the modern conceptions of uncon-scious motivation and of physiological, behavioural, and statistical analysis have only remote precursors before the second half of the nineteenth century.

Mental testing is the branch of modern psychology which is most obvious in its impact upon the classroom. Its para-phernalia of tests and statistical analyses are familiar. Its effects and implications have been the occasion of heated public controversy. To improve the assessment of human beings is such an intrinsically difficult and complex matter that layman and specialist alike can readily adopt extreme positions, either rejecting so-called psychometry in its entirety or claiming too much for the statistical analyses of test results. But educational and vocational choices have to be made in every community. The nature of the choices can be changed by changing the system, but the need to choose remains. Secondly, all systems of selection or choice are fallible; we cannot be sure even that we know what is best for ourselves. Consequently, while we can conceive in our minds of an ideal system, the practical problem is always to make improvements, not to leap to perfection. Thirdly, any person who is made responsible for the welfare of a large number of people is bound to make decisions which might be different if he had to think of only a few individuals. A parent may find two or three children an occasional strain on his attention, but a teacher, head-master, or senior administrator has to do his best for tens, hundreds, or thousands of children. Large numbers do not excuse any failure to respect individual people, but neither does respecting individuals excuse failure to use those techniques which help the achievement of the maximum all-round fairness. An understanding of statistical ideas is essential to teachers, whether the ideas are viewed as a part of ordinary logic or of educational control.

Child-study is the second psychological movement which has had an obvious influence on teachers. From it stem all the classroom methods, all the apparatus and text-books, associated with child-centred education. It embraces psychometric methods in their more directly applied aspects, especially in the use of tests to indicate the nature of an individual's capacities. Some of the pedagogic practices stemming from child-study are : the more careful grading of educational materials to match differing degrees of ability; the emphasis on activities, concrete objects, and pictures as valuable precursors or companions of the spoken or written word; and the greater attention paid to physical, emotional, and social education as being the complements of intellectual education. Child-study could advance only by being analytic, but its practitioners have also tried to remind us that each individual functions as a whole person, and as a whole person in a society; not as an I.Q. plus a set of endocrine secretions plus so many repressions, etc.

Mental health is the third major study in order of direct relevance to the classroom. It stresses the significance of personal relationships at the emotional level. It has made clear the inadequacy of any purely, or perhaps even mainly, intellectual account of human development. Its extreme supporters have sometimes seemed to dispossess the intellect altogether. This would, of course, give their own arguments the status of exhortations rather than proofs. Extremism aside, the many explorers and exponents of 'depth psychology' have made us aware of forces and mechanisms, frequently hidden, which can help or harm development, add to or detract from personal happiness. The origin of some of these forces has been convincingly connected with early and observable biological and social relationships, notably the relationship of maternal affection, physically expressed in a mother's care for her infant child. While the earlier psychology of the unconscious was misinterpreted to justify self-indulgence, current views increasingly support a philosophy of realistic unselfishness.

Social psychology is the fourth contributor to the teacher's outlook. It has two main aspects—the study of development in terms of intimate groups like the family, and in terms of wider social influences. It has entered into educational theory in the guise of 'socialized' education— that is, education in small groups and by co-operative methods. But the main educational force of social psychology is indirect. Its findings often encourage teachers to be more tolerant of things which they might otherwise blame or punish. It is salutary to recognize those features of a society that cannot be changed overnight even by a social revolution. It is also frustrating. Where ordinary school values are radically different from those prevailing in the surrounding social area, teachers have a trying job and deserve all the technical assistance and opportunities for discussing problems that can be provided.

Behaviourism and *physiological psychology* come fifth, for their bearing on the classroom is least direct. Behaviourism is both highly analytic and highly theoretical. The teacher cannot do much about the nervous system, the glandular balance, the complex patterning of reflexes, the genetic constitution, of a child in his class. But just as it is sometimes helpful in practice to take cognizance of the social limitations of education, so is it helpful to have regard to the physical frame which is the medium of all our highest endeavours. It has already been pointed out that the most exhaustive physiological analysis of our experience would not lessen experience as such. It would only modify the details of interpretation, just as we at present may make allowances for a person who is flushed with elation, anger, or embarrassment, or who is depressed by sickness, confused with alcohol, or deranged by a brain tumour. The behaviourist approach to human beings has encouraged people to explain human beings as far as possible in terms of what is elementary and observable. While this can be interpreted as an attempt to degrade mankind, it can also be interpreted as an attempt to clear the way for a true representation of what is distinctively human.

Educators have been extensively influenced by the kinds of psychological thinking that have just been recalled. Modern psychological ideas pervade their philosophy of education and their educational practice. The slogan "Education according to Nature," first popularized by

Rousseau, and developed by Pestalozzi, Froebel, and Dewey, has found much support in modern psychology. This philosophy of naturalism haunts the human mind. Can the study of the nature of the world and the men in it reveal the essence of the universe? Can one see the way that men *must* go and, by such insight, make the going easier? Idealist philosophers would deny that the mere existence of the way establishes any obligation to follow it. They would seek for such obligation in some source transcending the mundane world. This solution has its own problems. Here we are concerned only to remark upon the tendency for psychology, and, indeed, biology as a whole, to associate itself with a naturalist philosophy. Educators, even those most closely associated with naturalism, are readier to draw upon philosophic idealism. Nature offers so many ways; to select is to commit oneself to a kind of idealism.

Psychologists endeavour to be scientific: they observe and experiment and measure; they search for quantities and for precision; they want completeness and unification so far as their data allow. They can succeed in such aims most readily with simpler or elementary psychological phenomena. When they launch into the study of psychological complexities the observations are less consistent, the experiments are fewer, the data are increasingly intractable. This does not matter. The psychologist believes in his approach and looks forward to the maturity of his science. For the educator such patience is more difficult. He is embroiled in the complexities of human behaviour and in the practical demands of society. Such demands may tempt the educator to throw scientific method overboard. Its theories are 'materialistic' or 'mechanical' and not suited to the spiritual, non-mechanical nature of persons. This depends on whether the scientists are 'good' or 'bad' scientists. The scientific psychologist and the practical educator will see eye to eye if both are genuinely alive to the problems of the people around them. Either may become set in unfruitful attitudes if he sacrifices his questing mind on the altar of a fixed theory or practice.

Psychologists are determinists in so far as they try to demonstrate the observable causes of all behaviour; and yet they are associated with various doctrines of 'freedom' in education. Educators are anti-determinist in so far as they often emphasize the spontaneity and inexplicability of behaviour at its most human; and yet they are associated with the assertion of ideals, the maintenance of traditional standards, and even with authoritarian attitudes. Whatever freedom is, people think it is, on the whole, a good thing to have. The kinds of freedom that psychologists, and many educators, have advocated are (a) freedom from being directed into a single narrow channel of development so that other valuable channels are shut off; (b) freedom from such moral or academic standards as a child of a given age and ability cannot reasonably be expected to attain; (c) freedom from the tyranny of unrecognized mental conflicts which, because they are not recognized, burst out in unorthodox and sometimes harmful ways; and (d) freedom from the general influences of adults who are themselves immature or seriously repressed. Some educators would object to these freedoms. They might urge that there is only one way for each individual, that the educator's job is to maintain and raise standards, that mental ill-health is rare and mental conflict part of the essence of growing up and of living.

There may be differences of emphasis from one thinker to the next, but many of these differences are verbal. They are also based on not distinguishing between what is good to know and what is good to do. It is good for the teacher to know that Peter has an I.Q. of 75 and is not intellectually bright, but the teacher's art requires that he stimulate

Peter to do as much as he can. The full realization of intellectual potentiality must be sought at all levels. Progress in a task of any duration may require single-mindedness to the point of excluding rival interests, but the teacher should know when to 'let up' on such exclusive perseverance. Much mental conflict is unavoidable, a little repression may be of no consequence, and a considerable degree of queerness can be tolerated. But again, to recognize these happenings does not justify encouraging them.

Both education and psychology are relatively new as subjects of professional study. They have not had the prestige of subjects that have been established for very much longer, or that are more precise and scientific in their nature. Despite this, education and psychology, and the still less certain hybrid, educational psychology, represent a response to a range of phenomena and of problems that are very real for those who are responsible for the educational tasks of a community. In this sphere one may admit, borrowing the words of Lippmann (1955), that "there is a hiatus between the highest wisdom and the actual perplexities with which men deal." This need not have too serious consequences if, at each level of the educational hierarchy, respect is encouraged for the differing problems and the best efforts of those at other levels. The study of educational psychology can put some useful techniques in the hands of the teacher and the educational administrator. A knowledge of the general significance of these techniques is indispensable to practical educational discussion, although the need for a mastery of details is dependent on the nature of one's daily job. Educational psychology also offers a humanitarian approach to living or working with children. Even when the humanitarian impulse is already there it may be given a more helpful direction, just as the desire to rescue a drowning man is given actuality by the rescuer's ability to swim. What educational psychology does not do is to give us, by itself, the attitude or way of life that makes people fundamentally humane. Living with people is the main potential source of humanizing oneself. Reading in the great literature of the world, or having the good fortune to study under a great living person, is the second source of humanity and understanding. Without these, educational psychology as a purely academic study would do more harm than good.

Bibliography

MAINLY books that have contributed directly to the present text are listed. Those that might prove a moderately easy next step into various topics are starred. Schonell, perhaps, represents educational psychology in its most lucid applied form. Burt is a standard authority, copious but clear. Gesell's many studies of child development in the United States are valuable for reference. Piaget is another prolific writer on child development: his approach is individual and not easy for a beginner. Valentine is very human and balanced and writes from an English background. P. E. Vernon gives good reviews of the findings of experimental psychology. The National Book League published in 1956 a useful little bibliography of Child Psychology by Dr Edna Balint (2s. 6d.).

In the field of modern research important references are (a) the publications of the Scottish Council for Research in Education; (b) the publications of the National Foundation for Educational Research in England and Wales; and (c) the *British Journal of Educational Psychology*.

ADRIAN, E. D.: *The Physical Background of Perception* (Clarendon Press, 1947).

ADVISORY COUNCIL ON EDUCATION IN SCOTLAND: *Pupils who are Maladjusted because of Social Handicaps* (H.M.S.O., Edinburgh, 1952).

ALLPORT, G.: *Personality: a Psychological Interpretation* (Constable, 1938).

BALLARD, P. B.: *The New Examiner* (Hodder and Stoughton, 1923).

BARTLETT, F. C.: *Remembering* (Cambridge University Press, 1932).

BEVERIDGE, W. I. B.: *The Art of Scientific Investigation* (Heinemann, 1950).

BOWLBY, J.: *Maternal Care and Mental Health* (World Health Organization, Geneva, 1951).

*Child Care and the Growth of Love (Penguin Books, 1953).

BREW, J. M.: *Youth and Youth Groups* (Faber, 1957).

BROWN, J. A. C.: *The Social Psychology of Industry* (Penguin Books, 1954).

BURN, M.: **Mr. Lyward's Answer* (Hamilton, 1956).

BURT, SIR CYRIL: *The Young Delinquent* (University of London Press, 1925; 4th edition, 1944).

The Backward Child (University of London Press, 1937; 3rd edition, 1950).

The Causes and Treatment of Backwardness (University of London Press, 2nd edition, 1953).

"The Evidence for the Concept of Intelligence" (*British Journal of Educational Psychology*, 1955, vol. 25, p. 158).

CAMERON, N.: *The Psychology of Behaviour Disorders* (Houghton Mifflin, New York, 1947).

CARMICHAEL, L. (editor): *Manual of Child Psychology* (Chapman and Hall, 2nd edition, 1954).

Citizens of Tomorrow (published for the Council of the King George's Jubilee Trust) (Odhams Press, 1955).

CLARK, M.: *Left-handedness* (published for the Scottish Council for Research in Education) (University of London Press, 1957).

CLEUGH, M. F.: *The Slow Learner* (Methuen, 1957).

COLE, L. E.: *General Psychology* (McGraw-Hill, London, 1939).

CORNFORD, F. M.: *The Republic of Plato* (Clarendon Press, 1941).

Criminal Statistics, England and Wales, 1958 (H.M.S.O., London, 1959).

CRONBACH, L. J.: *Educational Psychology* (Harcourt, Brace, New York, 1954).

DEWEY, J.: *Democracy and Education* (Macmillan, New York, 1916).

Experience and Education (Macmillan, New York, 1938).

DOBINSON, C. H.: *Technical Education for Adolescents* (Harrap, 1951).

Early Leaving (a report of the Central Advisory Council for Education) (H.M.S.O., London, 1954).

EYSENCK, H. J.: *The Scientific Study of Personality* (Routledge and Kegan Paul, 1952).

The Structure of Human Personality (Methuen, 1953).

*Uses and Abuses of Psychology (Penguin Books, 1953).

FORD, D.: *The Deprived Child and the Community* (Constable, 1955).

FREUD, S.: *Psychopathology of Everyday Life* (originally published, 1914; Penguin Books edition, 1938).

*The Interpretation of Dreams (edited and translated by J. Strachey) (Allen and Unwin, 1955).

GALTON, F.: *Hereditary Genius* (originally published, 1869; Watts, 1950—reprint of 2nd edition of 1892).

GARDNER, D. E. M.: *Testing Results in the Infant School* (Methuen, 1942).

Long Term Results of Infant School Methods (Methuen, 1950).

GESELL, A.: "The Ontogenesis of Infant Behaviour" (Chapter VI of *Manual of Child Psychology*, 1954).

GESELL, A., ILG, F. L., AND AMES, L. B.: *Youth, the Years from Ten to Sixteen* (Hamilton, 1956).

GHISELLI, E. E., AND BROWN, C. W.: *Personnel and Industrial Psychology* (McGraw-Hill, New York, 2nd edition, 1955).

GILBRETH, F. B., AND CAREY, E. G.: *Cheaper by the Dozen* (Heinemann, 1949).

GITTINS, J.: *Approved School Boys* (H.M.S.O., London, 1952).

GLUECK, S. AND E.: *Unraveling Juvenile Delinquency* (The Commonwealth Fund, New York, 1950).

GRAY, W. S.: **The Teaching of Reading and Writing* (Evans, for UNESCO, 1956).

HALL, S. S.: *Adolescence* (Appleton, New York, 1904).

HARDING, D. W.: *Social Psychology and Individual Values* (Hutchinson's University Library, 1953).

HARRIS, H.: *The Group Approach to Leadership Testing* (Routledge and Kegan Paul, 1949).

HARTOG, SIR P., AND RHODES, E. C.: *The Marks of Examiners* (Macmillan, 1936).
An Examination of Examinations (Macmillan, 1936).

HEALY, W.: *The Individual Delinquent* (Little, Brown, Boston, 1915).

HILL, M. E.: *The Education of Backward Children* (Harrap, 1939).

HOLLINGSHEAD, A. B.: *Elmtown's Youth* (Wiley, New York, 1942)·

HOLLOWAY, J.: *Language and Intelligence* (Macmillan, 1951).

HOME OFFICE: "The Administration of Children's Home Regulations, 1951"—Reproduced in the Seventh Report on the Work of the Children's Department (H.M.S.O., London, 1955).

HULL, C. L.: *Principles of Behaviour* (Appleton-Century, New York, 1943).

HUME, D.: *A Treatise of Human Nature* (originally published, 1739).

HURLOCK, E.: *Adolescent Development* (McGraw-Hill, London, 1949; 2nd edition 1955).

HUXLEY, J.: *The Uniqueness of Man* (Chatto and Windus, 1941).

ISAACS, S.: *Social Development in Young Children* (Routledge, 1933).

JAMES, W.: *Psychology, Briefer Course* (Macmillan, 1892).
Talks to Teachers on Psychology (Longmans, Green, 1899; reprinted 1946).

Junior Secondary Education (published for the Scottish Education Department) (H.M.S.O., Edinburgh, 1955).

KINSEY, A. C.: *Sexual Behaviour in the Human Male* (Saunders, London, 1948).
Sexual Behaviour in the Human Female (Saunders, London, 1953).

KNIGHT, R.: *Intelligence and Intelligence Tests* (Methuen, 1933; 2nd edition, 1943).

KÖHLER, W.: *The Mentality of Apes* (Kegan Paul, 1925).

KUHLEN, R. G.: *The Psychology of Adolescent Development* (Harper, New York, 1952).

KUO, Z. Y.: "The nature of unsuccessful acts and their order of elimination in animal learning" (*Journal of Comparative Psychology*, 1922, vol. 2, p. 1). (Cited by Cole, 1939.)

LACK, D.: *The Life of the Robin* (Penguin Books, 1953).

LASHLEY, K. S.: *Brain Mechanisms and Intelligence* (University of Chicago Press, 1929).

LEWIN, K.: "Behaviour and Development as a Function of the Total Situation" (Chapter XV of *Manual of Child Psychology*, 1954).

LIPPMANN, W.: *The Public Philosophy* (Hamilton, 1955).

LLOYD, F.: *Educating the Sub-normal Child* (Methuen, 1953).

LOWENFELD, M.: **Play in Childhood* (Gollancz, 1935).

McDOUGALL, W.: *Introduction to Social Psychology* (Methuen, 1908; 24th edition, 1942).

McLAREN, V. M.: "Socio-economic Status and Reading Ability"—*Studies in Reading*, vol. II (Scottish Council for Research in Education, 1950).

MAIER, N. R. F.: "Reasoning in Humans" (*Journal of Comparative Psychology*, 1931, vol. 12, p. 181). (Cited by Cole, 1939.)

MANNHEIM, H., AND WILKINS, L. T.: *Prediction Methods in Relation to Borstal Training* (H.M.S.O., London, 1955).

MASSERMAN, J. H.: *Principles of Dynamic Psychiatry* (Saunders, London, 1946).

MEAD, M.: *The American Character* (Penguin Books, 1944).

MINISTRY OF EDUCATION: *Report of the Committee on Maladjusted Children* (H.M.S.O., London, 1955).

MORENO, J. L.: *Who Shall Survive?* (Beacon House, New York, 2nd edition, 1953).

MORLEY, D. W.: *The Ant World* (Penguin Books, 1953).

MORRIS, B.: "Mental Health in the Classroom"—from *The Bearings of Recent Advances in Psychology on Educational Problems* (University of London Institute of Education, 1955).

MUNN, N. L.: *Psychology: the Fundamentals of Human Adjustment* (Harrap, 3rd edition, 1956).

MYERS, C. S.: *Experimental Psychology* (Cambridge University Press, 3rd edition, 1925).

NATIONAL SOCIETY FOR THE STUDY OF EDUCATION: *Nature and Nurture*, 2 vols. (Public School Publishing Co., Illinois, 1928).

NEWMAN, H. H., FREEMAN, F. N., AND HOLZINGER, K. J.: *Twins: a Study of Heredity and Environment* (University of Chicago Press, 1937).

NOTCUTT, B.: **The Psychology of Personality* (Methuen, 1953).

NUNN, P.: *Education: Its Data and First Principles* (Arnold, 1920; 3rd edition, 1945).

OAKLEY, C. A.: *Men at Work (Hodder and Stoughton, and University of London Press, 1945).

PEARCE, J. D. W.: *Juvenile Delinquency* (Cassell, 1952).

PEEL, E. A.: footnote on "Practice Effects between Three Consecutive Tests of Intelligence" (*British Journal of Educational Psychology*, 1953, vol. 23, p. 126).
The Psychological Basis of Education (Oliver and Boyd, Edinburgh, 1956).

PENROSE, L.: *The Biology of Mental Defect* (Sidgwick and Jackson, 1949).

ROUSSEAU, J. J.: *Emile* (originally published, 1762).

SCHONELL, F. J.: *Backwardness in the Basic Subjects* (Oliver and Boyd, Edinburgh, 1942).
**The Psychology and Teaching of Reading* (Oliver and Boyd, Edinburgh, 1945).

SCHONELL, F. J. AND F. E.: **Diagnostic and Attainment Testing* (Oliver and Boyd, Edinburgh, 1950).
Diagnosis and Remedial Teaching in Arithmetic (Oliver and Boyd, Edinburgh, 2nd edition, 1957).

SCOTTISH COUNCIL FOR RESEARCH IN EDUCATION: *Studies in Reading* (University of London Press, 1950).
Social Implications of the 1947 Scottish Mental Survey (University of London Press, 1953).

SHERIF, M.: *An Outline of Social Psychology* (Harper, New York, 1948).

SLADE, P.: *Child Drama* (University of London Press, 1954).

STAFFORD-CLARK, D.: *Psychiatry Today* (Penguin Books, 1952).

STAGNER, R., AND KARWOSKI, T. F.: *Psychology* (McGraw-Hill, New York, 1952).

STOTT, D. H.: *Saving Children from Delinquency* (University of London Press, 1952).
Unsettled Children and their Families (University of London Press, 1956).

SULLY, J.: *Studies of Childhood* (Longmans, Green, 1895).

TAYLOR, C. D.: "The Effect of Training on Reading Readiness"—*Studies in Reading*, vol. II (Scottish Council for Research in Education, 1950).

TERMAN, L., AND MERRILL, M. A.: *Measuring Intelligence* (Harrap, 1937).

TERMAN, L., AND ODEN, M. H.: *The Gifted Child Grows Up* (Stanford University Press, 1947).

THYNE, J. M.: *Patterns of Error in the Addition Number Facts* (University of London Press, 1954).

Times Educational Supplement: "Understanding the Spoken Word" (May 11, 1951).

TREDGOLD, A. F. AND F. F.: *Mental Deficiency* (Baillière, Tindall, and Cox; 8th edition, 1952).

UNDERWOOD, J. E. A. (Chairman): *Report of the Committee on Maladjusted Children* (H.M.S.O., London, 1956).

UNIVERSITY OF LONDON INSTITUTE OF EDUCATION: *The Bearings of Recent Advances in Psychology on Educational Problems* (Evans, 1955).

VALENTINE, C. W.: *The Reliability of Examinations* (University of London Press, 1932).
The Normal Child (Penguin Books, 1956).

VENABLES, P. F. R.: *Technical Education* (Bell, 1955).

VERNON, M. D.: *Backwardness in Reading* (Cambridge University Press, 1957).

VERNON, P. E.: *The Structure of Human Abilities* (Methuen, 1950).
Personality Tests and Assessments (Methuen, 1953).
The Measurement of Abilities (University of London Press, 2nd edition, 1956).

Secondary School Selection (edited for the British Psychological Society) (Methuen, 1957).

WALL, W. D.: *Education and Mental Health* (Harrap, for UNESCO, 1955).

WALTER, W. G.: *The Living Brain* (Duckworth, 1953).

WARNER, W. L., HAVIGHURST, R. J., AND LOEB, M. L.: *Who shall be Educated?* (Kegan Paul, 1946).

WATTS, A. F.: *The Language and Mental Development of Children* (Harrap, 1944).

YATES, A.: "The Effects of Coaching and Practice in Intelligence Tests" (*British Journal of Educational Psychology*, 1953, vol. 23, p. 147).

ZIEMER, G.: *Education for Death* (Constable, 1942).

Index

ACADEMIC success, and I.Q., 63;
and occupational class, 207
Adolescence, physiological changes
in, 132, 154–156; emotional
development in, 156–159; social
life in, 159–161; intellectual
development in, 161–162; need
for guidance in, 162–163; in-
stinct in, 195
Adoption, 108
Ambivalence, 169
Animal learning, 19–25
Anxiety, 62, 139–140, 169, 174,
192
Approved schools, 106
Archetypes, 140
Arithmetic, 25, 32, 35–37, 76, 85,
88, 90, 114
Art, 112–116
Attainment quotients, 74, 83
Attendance centres, 106
Autonomic nervous system, 188,
191, 197

BACKWARDNESS, and intelligence,
62, 64, 83, 85; definition of,
83; general, 84–85; specific,
85–87; treatment of, 86–94;
home influence on, 88–89; in
reading, 91–93
Bartlett, F. C., 40–43
Behaviourism, 24, 27, 176, 192,
195, 214
Binet, A., 10, 49
Biological criteria of success, 180–
181
Biology, 25
Biosphere, 141, 146
Borstals, 106–107
Bowlby, J., 107

Burt, Sir Cyril, 10, 47, 49, 50,
51, 54, 62, 84, 85, 101–103

CENTRAL nervous system, 22, 61,
147, 188–191
Cerebral cortex, 189
Certification, 61
Character, 129, 164
Child, -study, 11, 212–213; -guid-
ance, 15, 86, 94, 168, 174–175;
care, 107–109; drama, 116–118
Children Act (1908), 105
Children Act (1948), 107
Children and Young Persons Act
(1933), 105
Children's homes, 101, 108
Chromosomes, 143, 183, 186, 188
Colchester Survey, 61
Common curriculum, 206
Compensation, 173
Conditioned learning, 20–22
Control groups, 84, 102, 103
Correlation, 75–78, 80–81
Creative activity, 113–116
Cretin, 192
Culture pattern, 206
Curriculum, and methods, 28, 30,
35, 38, 96; adapting of, 164;
common, 206

DARWIN, C., 184
Delinquency, various views of,
101–104; treatment of, 102–
103; and the law, 105–107;
and repression, 172; and films,
207
Depression, 174
Deprivation, 107
Depth psychology, 138, 213
Detention centres, 106

Determinism, 216

Development, social, 34, 99, 103–104, 117–118, 198–199, 213; intellectual, 51–53, 161–162; emotional, 107, 113–118, 144, 150–151, 156–161, 168–169; sexual, 140, 154–156; Gesell's principles of, 145–147; early language, 148–149; adolescent, 155–162

Developmental direction, Gesell's principles of, 145–147

Dewey, J., 198–199, 215

Diagnostic methods, in arithmetic, 36, 91–92; for specific backwardness, 86; in reading, 91–92, 125–126; for delinquency, 102–104; in psychoanalysis, 139; in leadership testing, 200

Discipline, theory of mental, 38; and the young teacher, 96–101, 109–110; free, 97; parental, 99–100; teacher's experience of, 100; and delinquency, 102; and home background, 109; through drama, 117; self-, 150; and repression, 172

Dominant genetic traits, 184–185

Dreams, 139, 150, 171

Drive, concept of, 22, 86

Dullness, intellectual, 51, 62, 64, 85

Ectomorphy, 130–131

Educable mental defectives, 62

Educational, guidance, 63, 165; age, 73–74

Educationally sub-normal children, 62, 63, 64, 82

Eduction of relationships and correlates, 47

Effort after meaning, 40

Ego, 138, 168

Ego-involvement, 124

Electro-encephalography, 190–191

Emotional blockage, 43

Emotional development, in delinquents, 103–104; in infancy and childhood, 107, 144, 168–169; through æsthetic activity, 113–116; through drama, 116–118; through play, 150–151; in adolescence, 156–161

Endocrine glands, 131–132, 188, 191–192, 197

Endomorphy, 130–131

English, 23, 27, 32, 69, 76, 85, 86, 93, 112, 115, 118, 162, 166

English Mental Survey (1927), 60

Environment, problem of heredity and, 30, 45, 52, 185–188; physical, 181–182; physiological, 182

Examinations, as a goal, 21; reliability of, 66–67; and æsthetic development, 115; and general education, 152–153

Extraversion, 130, 132–133

Eysenck, H. J., 133, 177, 187–188

Factorial analysis, of tests of ability, 47–48; general significance of, 78–79

Family Service Units, 109

Family size, 205

Fantasy, 150, 168, 169–170

Feeble-minded, 51, 59–60, 61

Finchden Manor School, 98

Fixation, visual, 125; developmental, 140

Forgetting, 139

Foster homes, 107, 108

Free association, 139, 203

Free discipline, 97

Freedom in education, 19, 97–98, 216

Freud, S., 39, 138, 140, 155–156, 168–169, 171, 177, 203

Frontal lobes, 190

Functional asymmetry, 146

Functional autonomy, 197

Galton's law of regression, 58

Genes, 183–186, 188

Genetics, 183–186

Geography, 23, 26, 27, 37

Gesell, A., 10, 52, 145–148, 158

Gestalt psychology, 24–27; and intelligence, 48; and backwardness, 87

Gifted children and adults, 55–59, 64–65
Guidance, child-, 15, 86, 94, 168, 174–175; vocational, 31, 63, 119–121

HABIT, W. James on, 33
Halo effect, 136
Heredity, problem of environment and, 30, 45, 52, 185–188; operation of, 183–185
History, 23, 37, 67
Home background, and school success, 30, 207; and intelligence, 54, 57; and backwardness, 88–89; and delinquency, 102, 104; conflicting influences of, 108; and discipline, 109
Homosexual phase, 155–156
Hormic psychology, 196
Hume, D., 38
Hypochondria, 172

Id, 138, 168
Idealism, 153, 215
Identification, 173
Idiot, 51, 59, 60, 61
Imbecile, 51, 59, 60, 61
Independence, training for, 126
Individual differences, 14–15, 28–31, 37, 47, 122
Individuality, value of, 13, 15
Individuating maturation, 146–147
Infant development, 143–153; Freudian view of, 139–140, 168–169
Inferiority feelings, 140
Instinct theory, 194–195
Intellectual development, early, 114; adolescent, 161–162
Intelligence, nature of, 11–12, 45–49; and scholastic success, 30, 46, 57–58, 63, 76–78; factorial analysis of, 47–48; defective, 51, 59–63; adult, 52; inherited and acquired, 52–55, 187; and socio-economic status, 54–55, 57, 187; high, 56–59, 64–65, 76–78; and backwardness, 83–85; and deprivation,

107; and vocational guidance, 120; and reading, 125; of twins, 187; and electro-encephalography, 190–191
Intelligence quotients, normal distribution of, 50–51, 72–73; calculation of, 71–72, 74
Intelligence tests, 49–53; objectivity of, 53, 81; reliability and validity of, 80
Interest, arousal of, 33–34, 87–88, 115–116, 118, 124, 204
Interviews, 67, 135
Introversion, 130, 132–133

JAMES, W., 10, 33, 39

KINESTHETIC stimuli, 22
Kohs' Block Design test, 50

LANGUAGE development, 36, 148–149
Languages, 23, 24, 25, 26, 34, 43, 76, 112
Leadership, 199–201
Learning, 18–38; animal, 19–25; maze, 19, 21–24; conditioned, 20–22; reward in, 20–22, 31–35, 88, 98; trial-and-error, 23–24; transfer of, 23, 37–38; and motivation, 23, 28, 31–35; behaviourist and *Gestalt* views of, 24, 27; by insight, 25, 27; and organization of curricula and methods, 28–31, 35–37; and individual differences, 28–31; to read, 29, 36, 91, 124–126; and habit, 33; and enthusiasm, 33–35; by modern methods, 34; sense of reality in, 37; of skills, 121–126; curve of, 122–123
Left-handedness, 146
Locke, J., 211

McDOUGALL, W., 10, 194–196
Maladjustment, 64, 104, 174–175, 181
Marking, 66–71, 137
Mass media, 207
Maternal care, 104, 107, 144, 210, 213

Mathematics, 21, 24, 37–38, 67, 76
Maturation, 143, 147
Maze learning, 19, 21–24
Mean score, 68, 70, 72
Median, 69
Memorizing, traditional place of, 18, 19; and word-meanings, 39; improved methods of, 43
Memory, 38–44
Mendel, G., 183–185
Mental, measurement, 13; age, 36, 49, 52, 71–72, 74; testing, 49–53, 73–75, 86, 211–212; deficiency, 51–52, 59–63, 82; disorder, 62, 174; conflict, 139–140, 160, 168–169, 216, 217; health, 167–178, 213, 216
Mental Survey, English (1927), 60; Scottish (1933), 60; Scottish (1947), 56, 187, 205
Mesomorphy, 130–131
Methods, of study, 7, 18, 43, 121–122; psychometric, 49–53, 86, 134–138, 211–212; statistical, 68–71
Methods of teaching, 30–37; co-operative, 34, 198–199; for backward children, 86–95; and discipline, 97–98, 109; skills, 121–126; for primary schools, 152–153; for adolescents, 166
Moral defectives, 60
Moreno, J. L., 201–204
Motivation, and learning, 23, 28, 31–35; physiological and social, 197
Music, 26, 115
Mutation, 185

National Institute of Industrial Psychology, 120
National Society for the Study of Education, 54
Natural selection, 184
Naturalism, 153, 214–215
Nerve impulse, 22, 190
Nervous system, central, 22, 61, 147, 188–191; autonomic, 188, 191, 197
Neurosis, 133, 174, 177, 188; in animals, 176

Normal distribution, of I.Q.'s, 50–51; curve of, 72–73; of ratings, 137

Objectivity of tests, 53, 81
Occupation and intelligence, 55–57, 120, 187
Organic psychosis, 176

Paranoia, 174
Parents, intelligence of, 58; anxiety caused by, 89; discipline by, 99–100; children unwanted by, 104; and infant development, 144, 169, 213; adolescent conflict with, 160, 162
Pavlov, I. P., 19–21
Peer culture, adolescent, 159, 161
Personality, assessment of, 12–13, 90, 134–138; definition of, 129; uniqueness of, 129, 134; and typology, 129–131, 132–134; and the endocrine glands, 131–132; Freudian view of, 138–140; emotional and social aspects of, 167
Phonic analysis, 91, 93, 112, 126
Physique, and intelligence, 15, 57, 205; and personality, 129–131
Plato, 46–47
Play, 149–151
Play-way, 15, 150
Practice in learning, 19, 21–23, 122–123, 124–125, 147
Prägnanz, law of, 24
Probation, 105
Projection, 114, 139, 173; tests, 135–136
Projects, 34, 164, 198
Propaganda, 19, 201
Psychiatric social workers, 175
Psychiatry, 175, 177
Psychoanalysis, 138–140, 203; criticism of, 177
Psychodrama, 203
Psychogalvanic skin response, 134
Psychometric methods, 49–53, 86, 134–138, 211–212
Psychoneuroses, 177

Psychotherapy, 93, 139, 140, 172–173, 177–178, 203
Psychoticism, 133, 170
Punishment, corporal, 8, 96–97, 101; in school, 19, 31, 35, 87, 204

RANDOM sample, 79
Ratings, of gifted persons, 58; of physique, 130; distribution of, 136–137; of personality traits, 136–138
Rationalization, 41, 42, 173
Raven's Matrices, 50
Reading, readiness for, 29, 36, 64, 86, 124, 147; and socio-economic status, 30; age, 73–74; diagnostic tests in, 91–92; backwardness in, 91–93; psychology of learning, 124–126
Reciprocal interweaving, 146
Regression, 173; Galton's law of, 58
Regulatory fluctuation, 147
Reinforcement, 14, 22
Reliability of assessments, 53, 80, 135
Remand homes, 105–106
Remedial teaching, 92–94
Representative sample, 11, 53, 72, 79
Repression, 39, 171–173, 216, 217
Retardation, 52, 74–75, 83–84
Reward in learning, 20–22, 31–35, 88, 98
Rorschach test, 135–136
Rousseau, J. J., 8, 47, 112, 210–211, 215
'R's,' three, 29, 51, 88, 112, 147, 162

SAMPLING, statistical, 11, 53, 72, 79
Scaling, 69–71
Schizophrenia, 174
Scholastic abilities and intelligence, 30, 46, 57–58, 63, 76–78
Schonell, F. J., 10, 85–86, 91, 93
Schools, grammar, 30, 67, 164; primary, 46, 94, 145, 149, 152;

secondary, 46, 65, 118, 127, 154, 157, 164, 206, 207; high, 56; E.S.N., 62, 63, 64; approved, 105, 106
Science, 27
Scottish Council for Research in Education, 10, 56
Scottish Mental Survey (1933), 60; (1947), 56, 187, 205
Sentiments, 144, 195
Sexual development, 140, 154–156
Significance, statistical, 79, 81
Sign-learning theory, 23
Skill, acquisition of, 12, 18, 29, 121–126; teaching, 23, 36, 113; value of, 116; in language, 148–149; social, 159
Slade, P., 116–118
Social development, through class methods, 34, 99, 198–199, 213; of delinquents, 103–104; through drama, 117–118; earliest, 144; and language, 149; through play, 149; in adolescence, 159–161, 207; through functional autonomy of social motives, 197; through psychodrama, 203
Social psychology, 213–214
Socializing education, 34, 198–199, 213
Socio-economic status, and reading, 30; and intelligence, 54–55, 57, 187
Sociogram, 202
Sociological aspects of education, 205–208
Sociometry, 201–204
Spearman, C., 47
Specific backwardness, 85–87
Spontaneity, 203
Standard deviation, 68, 70, 72
Standard error, 79
Standardized tests, 15, 71–73
Statistical methods, 11, 67–81
Subtraction methods, 35–36
Super-ego, 138

TEACHERS, professional education of, 7–8, 32, 43, 85, 87, 100, 128, 168, 178, 217–218

Teaching methods, traditional, 19; and animal experiments, 23–24; and motivation, 23, 28, 31–35; and *Gestalt* psychology, 25–27; and individual differences, 28–31; group, 29; infant, 34; in arithmetic, 35–36; and modern aids, 37; and remembering, 43; and intelligence, 64–65; for backward children, 85–94; and discipline, 98, 109; child-centred, 113–114, 152–153, 164; examination-centred, 115–116, 152–153, 165; selection as part of, 120; for imparting skills, 121–127; and the play-way, 150; economics of, 152; co-operative, 198–199

Technical education, liberalizing of, 118; and the psychology of learning, 119; selection for, 120–121; methods in, 121–127

Temperament, 13, 129, 134; instability of, 102; and physique, 131

Terman, L., 49, 56–59, 64

Terman-Merrill test, 49, 52

Test construction, 49–53, 71–73

Thematic Apperception Test, 136

Thorndike, E. L., 21–22

Time-and-motion study, 125

Tonic neck reflex, 146

Topological psychology, 141

Toys, 151

Transfer of training, 23, 37–38

Trial-and-error learning, 23, 24

Twins, 147, 186–188

Typology, 129–131, 132–134

Unconscious, the, 138, 175, 213

Uniqueness of man, 193

Validity of assessments, 53, 80, 135

Variance of marks or scores, 68, 70

Vernon, P. E., 132–133, 135, 136–137

Vocational, education, 118–121; guidance, 120–121